Collins | English for Exams

Cambridge English Qualifications

A2 Key
for Schools

2

8 practice tests

T0340568

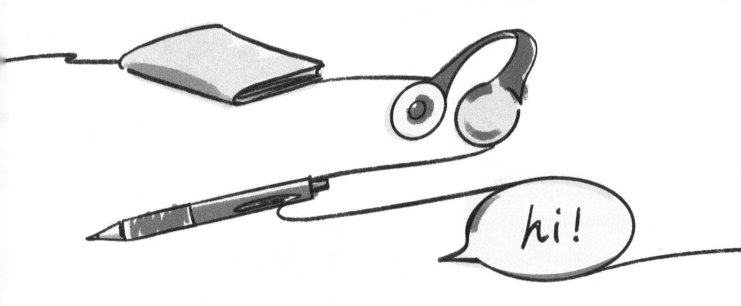

Published by Collins
An imprint of HarperCollins Publishers
Westerhill Road
Bishopbriggs
Glasgow
G64 2QT

HarperCollins Publishers
Macken House
39/40 Mayor Street Upper
Dublin 1
D01 C9W8
Ireland

First edition 2022

10 9 8 7 6 5 4

© HarperCollins Publishers 2022

ISBN 978-0-00-848416-3

Collins® and COBUILD® are registered trademarks of
HarperCollins Publishers Limited

collins.co.uk/elt

A catalogue record for this book is available from the
British Library.

If you would like to comment on any aspect of this book,
please contact us at the given address or online.
E-mail: collins.elt@harpercollins.co.uk

Authors: Patrick McMahon
Series editor: Celia Wigley
For the Publisher: Lisa Todd, Gillian Bowman and Kerry
Ferguson
Editor: Anastasia Vassilatou
Typesetter: Jouve, India
Illustrations: Jouve, India
Photographs: All photos from Shutterstock.com
Printer: Printed and bound by Ashford Colour
Press Ltd.
Audio recorded and produced by ID Audio, London
Cover designer: Gordon McGilp
Cover illustration: Maria Herbert-Liew
Sample Answer sheets (pages 194–7): Reproduced
with permission of Cambridge Assessment English ©
UCLES 2022

The Publishers gratefully acknowledge the permission
granted to reproduce the copyright material in this book.
Whilst every effort has been made to trace the copyright
holders, in cases where this has been unsuccessful, or if
any have inadvertently been overlooked, the Publishers
would gladly receive any information enabling them to
rectify any error or omission at the first opportunity.

All exam-style questions and sample answers in this
title were written by the authors.

About the author

Patrick McMahon is a university lecturer, teacher
trainer, materials writer and academic. He has taught
English in universities, colleges, secondary schools
and language schools in the UK, mainland Europe, Asia
and the Middle East. He has written a broad range of
materials for publishers and specialises in English for
Academic Purposes.

Contents

How to use this book

Who is this book for?

This book will help you to prepare for the *Cambridge Assessment English A2 Key for Schools* exam. The exam is also known as the *KET for Schools* exam. The exam was updated for 2020 and this book was written for the new exam. This book will be useful if you are preparing for the exam for the first time or taking it again. The book has been designed so that you can use it to study on your own, however, you can also use it if you are preparing for the *A2 Key for Schools* exam in a class.

The book contains:

- **Tips for success** – important advice to help you to do well in the exam
- **About A2 Key for Schools** – a guide to the exam
- **How to prepare for the test** – advice to help you to succeed in each part
- **Practice tests** – eight complete practice tests
- **Mini-dictionary** – definitions of the more difficult words from the practice tests
- **Audio scripts** – the texts of what you hear in the Listening and Speaking parts
- **Sample answer sheets** – make sure you know what the answer sheets look like
- **Answer key** – the answers for Reading and Listening
- **Model answers** – examples of good answers for the Writing and Speaking parts
- **Speaking: Additional practice by topic** – more sample questions to help you prepare for the Speaking test
- **Audio** – all the recordings for the practice tests as well as model answers for Speaking are available online at: www.collins.co.uk/eltresources

Tips for success

- **Start studying early** – The more you practise, the better your English will become. Give yourself at least two months to revise and complete all the practice tests in this book. Spend at least one hour a day studying.
- **Time yourself** when you do the practice tests. This will help you to feel more confident when you do the real exam.
- **Do every part** of each practice test. Don't be afraid to make notes in the book. For example, writing down the meaning of words you don't know on the page itself will help you to remember them later on.

Using the book for self-study

If you haven't studied for the *A2 Key for Schools* exam before, it is a good idea to do all the tests in this book in order. If you have a teacher or friend who can help you with your speaking and writing, that would be very useful. It is also a good idea to meet up with other students who are preparing for the exam or who want to improve their English. Having a study partner will help you to stay motivated. You can also help each other with areas of English you might find difficult.

Begin preparing for the *A2 Key for Schools* exam by getting to know the different parts of the exam, what each part tests and how many marks there are for each part. Use the information in the **About A2 Key for Schools** section to find out all you can. You can also download the *A2 Key for Schools Handbook* from the Cambridge Assessment English website for more details.

You need to know how to prepare for each of the parts of the exam in the best way possible. The **How to prepare for the test** section in this book will be useful. Try to follow the advice as it will help you to develop the skills you need.

In the practice tests in this book, you will see certain words highlighted in grey. These are the more difficult words and you can find definitions of these in the **Mini-dictionary** at the back of the book. The definitions are from *Collins COBUILD* dictionaries. It's a good idea to download the *Cambridge A2 Key*

Vocabulary List from the Cambridge Assessment English website. This is a list of words that you should understand at A2 level and the list is the same if you're taking the *A2 Key* test or the *A2 Key for Schools* test. Look through the list and make a note of the words you don't know. Then look up their meaning in a dictionary. You could use the Collins online dictionary: www.collinsdictionary.com. Knowing these words will help you to do better in the exam. Search 'A2 Key Vocabulary List 2020'.

Preparing for the Writing and Speaking parts

When you are ready to try the practice tests, make sure you answer the questions in the Writing parts as well as the Speaking parts. You can only improve your skills by practising a lot. Practise writing to a time limit. If you find this difficult at first, start by writing a very good answer of the correct length without worrying about time. Then try to complete your writing faster until you can write a good answer within the time limit. Learn to estimate the number of words you have written without counting them. Study the model answers at the back of the book. This will give you a clear idea of the standard your answers need to be. Don't try to memorise emails, notes or stories for the Writing part or answers to the questions in the Speaking part. If you work your way through the book, you should develop the skills and language you need to give good answers in the real exam.

The Speaking part in this book has accompanying audio so that you can practise answering the examiner's questions. You will be Candidate B, so if you hear the examiner ask Candidate B a question, this means you should answer by pausing the audio on your computer and answering the question. In Part 2 of the Speaking test, you are expected to have a conversation with Candidate A. Again, you will be Candidate B and will respond to Candidate A's statements or questions.

This experience will not be 100% authentic as Candidate A cannot respond to your statements or questions, however, this book and the audio have been designed to give you an excellent opportunity to practise answering questions through the eight practice tests. Once you have finished the Speaking part, you can listen to the model answers for Candidate B that have been provided for you. Another option is that you record your answers and then compare these with the model answers.

Please note that there are two versions of the Speaking Test audio:

- The first version contains the pauses for you to practise answering the questions in the Speaking tests. This is when you have to answer the questions for Candidate B. The scripts for this audio can be found from page 166 onwards in your book. For example, you'll see on page 168 that Test 1 Speaking audio track is labelled 'Track 06'. Look for Track 06 when you search for the audio online.
- The second version of the audio contains the Model Answers for the Speaking tests. These are for you to listen to, to see how a good student might answer the questions in the Speaking test. The scripts for this audio can be found from page 205 onwards in your book. You'll see that these audio files are labelled with an 'a' at the end, for example Track 06a, etc. Look for Track 06a when you search for the audio online.

At the back of the book you'll find more sample questions for the Speaking test. These provide another opportunity to practise answering questions that an examiner might ask you. There are 16 topics and all the questions have been recorded. Try answering these questions as fully as possible. Don't just give a 'yes/no' answer but try to give a reason or an example in your answer.

Finally, read as much as possible in English; this is the best way to learn new vocabulary and improve your English.

About A2 Key for Schools

The *Cambridge A2 Key for Schools* exam is a pre-intermediate-level English exam delivered by Cambridge Assessment English. It is for school students who need to show that they can deal with everyday English at a pre-intermediate level. In other words, you have to be able to:

- understand simple written information such as signs and notes
- write in simple English on everyday subjects
- show you can follow and understand a range of spoken materials such as announcements when people speak reasonably slowly
- show you can take part in different types of interactions using simple spoken English.

The exam is one of several offered by Cambridge Assessment English at different levels. The table below shows how *A2 Key for Schools* fits into the Cambridge English Qualifications. The level of this exam is described as being at A2 on the Common European Framework of Reference (CEFR).

	CEFR	Cambridge English Scale	Cambridge qualification
Proficient user	C2	200–230	C2 Proficiency
	C1	180–199	C1 Advanced
Independent user	B2	160–179	B2 First for Schools
	B1	140–159	B1 Preliminary for Schools
Basic user	A2	120–139	A2 Key for Schools
	A1	100–119	A1 Movers
	Pre-A1	80–99	Pre A1 Starters

The *A2 Key for Schools* qualification is for school students and it is an ideal first exam for those new to learning English and it gives learners confidence to study for higher Cambridge English Qualifications. Cambridge Assessment English also offers an *A2 Key* qualification. Both tests follow the same format and the candidates are tested in the same skills. However, the content of the exam is a bit different. The *A2 Key for Schools* is for candidates who are at school and is designed to suit the interests and experiences of school-age candidates. The *A2 Key* exam is for older students studying general English or those in higher education. If you are an adult learner, it would be better for you to take the *A2 Key* qualification and use the *Collins Practice Tests for A2 Key* to prepare for the exam.

There are three papers (or tests) in **A2 Key for Schools**:

- Paper 1: Reading and Writing (1 hour)
- Paper 2: Listening (approximately 30 minutes)
- Paper 3: Speaking (8–10 minutes)

Timetabling

You usually take the Reading and Writing test and the Listening test on the same day. The Speaking test may take place on a different day and it may be before or after the other tests. If you are studying on your own, you should contact your exam centre for dates. The exam is paper based. You can also take the exam on computer in some countries. For more information, see: https://www.cambridge-exams.ch/exams/CB_exams.php.

Paper/Test 1 Reading and Writing (1 hour)

Candidates need to be able to understand simple written information, such as signs and newspapers, and produce simple written English.

The **Reading and Writing** test has seven parts. Reading parts 1–5 have 30 questions and there is one mark for each question. Writing parts 6 and 7 have only one question each. Students should spend about 40 minutes on the Reading parts and about 20 minutes on the Writing parts of this test.

The Reading section has five parts.

Part 1 has six short emails, notices, signs or text messages. There are three sentences next to each one. You have to choose which sentence matches the meaning of the email, notice, sign or text message. (Total marks: 6)

Part 2 has seven questions and three short texts on the same topic. You have to match each question to one of the texts. (Total marks: 7)

Part 3 has a longer text, for example, a simplified newspaper or magazine article. There are five multiple-choice questions with three options: A, B and C. (Total marks: 5)

Part 4 has a short text with six numbered spaces. You decide which of the three words provided belongs in each gap. (Total marks: 6)

Part 5 has a short text with six gaps. You have to fill in six gaps in a text or texts using single words. (Total marks: 6)

The Writing section has two parts: Parts 6 and 7 of the Reading and Writing test.

In **Part 6** you write a short email or note. This should be 25 words or more. (Total marks: 15)

In **Part 7** you write a short story using picture prompts. This should be 35 words based on three picture prompts. (Total marks: 15)

In each part, marks are awarded in the following ways:
- five marks if you include all the necessary information
- five marks if you organise your message so a reader can follow it easily
- five marks if you use a good range of grammar structures and vocabulary.

Paper/Test 2 Listening (30 minutes)

Candidates need to show they can follow and understand a range of spoken materials, such as announcements, when people speak reasonably slowly.

The Listening test has five parts and there are 25 questions in total.

Part 1 has five short dialogues, for example, conversations at home or in a shop, and five questions. For each question, you have to listen and choose the correct answer from three options: A, B or C. The options are pictures. (Total marks: 5)

Part 2 has a longer text. You listen and write the missing information (prices, times, telephone numbers) in the gaps. You should write only one word, or a number, or a date, or a time for your answer. (Total marks: 5)

Part 3 has a longer informal conversation. You listen and choose the correct answer to a question from three options: A, B or C. The questions include opinions and attitudes of the speaker. (Total marks: 5)

Part 4 has five short conversations. You listen and choose the best answer from the three options: A, B or C. (Total marks: 5)

Part 5 has a longer conversation between two people who know each other. You match each of five items in the first list with five of the eight items in the second list. (Total marks: 5)

Paper/Test 3 Speaking (8–10 minutes)

Candidates take the Speaking test with another candidate or in a group of three. You are tested on your ability to take part in different types of interaction: with the examiner, with the other candidate and by yourself.

The Speaking test has two parts.

In **Part 1** the examiner asks you some questions about your name, where you live, your daily life, etc. and then the examiner asks you a longer 'Tell me something about ...' question. You respond to the examiner. (Time: 3–4 minutes)

In **Part 2**, the examiner gives you five pictures on a particular topic, e.g. hobbies. You talk together with the other candidate and discuss the activities, things or places in the pictures. After you have spoken for 1–2 minutes, the examiner continues the conversation by asking you questions related to the pictures. Then the examiner asks you two more questions on the same topic.
(Time: 4–6 minutes)

Marks and results

After the exam, all candidates receive a Statement of Results. Candidates whose performance ranges between CEFR Levels A1 and B1 (Cambridge English Scale scores of 100–150) also receive a certificate.

The Statement of Results shows the candidate's:

- score on the Cambridge English Scale for their performance in each of the four language skills (reading, writing, listening and speaking).
- score on the Cambridge English Scale for their overall performance in the exam. This overall score is the average of their scores for the four skills.
- grade – this is based on the candidate's overall score.
- level on the CEFR – this is also based on the overall score.

The certificate shows the candidate's:

- score on the Cambridge English Scale for each of the four skills.
- overall score on the Cambridge English Scale.
- grade.
- level on the CEFR.
- level on the UK National Qualifications Framework (NQF).

For *A2 Key for Schools*, the following scores will be used to report results:

Cambridge English Scale Score	Grade	CEFR Level
140–150	A	B1
133–139	B	A2
120–132	C	A2
100–119	Level A1	A1

Grade A: Cambridge English Scale scores of 140–150

Candidates sometimes show ability beyond Level A2. If a candidate achieves a Grade A in their exam, they will receive the *Key English Test for Schools* certificate stating that they demonstrated ability at Level B1.

Grades B and Grade C: Cambridge English Scale scores of 120–139

If a candidate achieves a Grade B or Grade C in their exam, they will receive the *Key English Test for Schools* certificate at Level A2.

CEFR Level A1: Cambridge English Scale scores of 100–119

If a candidate's performance is below Level A2, but falls within Level A1, they will receive a *Cambridge English* certificate stating that they demonstrated ability at Level A1.

Scores between 100 and 119 are also reported on your Statement of Results, but you will not receive a *Key English Test for Schools* certificate.

For more information on how the exam is marked, go to: http://www.cambridgeenglish.org

Working through the practice tests in this book will improve your exam skills, help you with timing for the exam, give you confidence and help you get a better result in the exam.

Good luck!

How to prepare for the test

This part of the book looks at each part of the test in detail. It describes common mistakes that students make, and suggests what you can do to improve your chances of doing well in that part.

Reading Part 1

In this part of the test, you read six short texts: signs, notices, phone texts or emails. There are three sentences about each text, and you have to choose the one that matches its meaning. Here is an example:

Hi Jane,

I'm sorry we can't meet as planned at break, but I'm free at lunchtime if you are.

Sue

A Sue wants to change her meeting time with Jane.

B Jane can't meet as planned, but she can meet Sarah at lunchtime.

C Sue is offering Jane a free lunch.

This part tests your understanding of different kinds of short texts. Read the text before you read the three sentences A–C. If the text is an email or phone text, think about who is writing it, who they are writing to, and what the relationship is between them. If the text is a sign or notice, think about where it is, and who it is for. Be careful: sentences often mix up the names of the people in an email or phone text, so a sentence might look right, but the wrong person says or does something, so the sentence is the wrong answer. Also, be careful if a sentence uses a lot of words from a text; the words might be the same, but they might be used to say something different. You have to find the sentence that has the same meaning as the text, but perhaps using different words.

In the example above, A is the correct answer. It gives the reason Sue sent the message, but it uses different words from the text.

COMMON MISTAKES: To choose an answer because it has the same words as the text. / To choose an answer which is nearly correct, but the names are mixed up.

YOU SHOULD: Check the names in the sentences carefully and think about who is writing the message and who is reading it. / Read signs and notices in English and short messages on social media. Do an IMAGE SEARCH with an internet search engine using the words 'school notices' and read the results. If you can, discuss these notices with a study partner.

Reading Part 2

In this part of the test, you read three texts about different people. Then you have to answer seven questions. The questions are usually about who does what. This part tests whether you can find the correct information quickly in a text and then understand the details.

First, read the texts for general understanding. Then read the first question and underline the key words. Next, read each text quickly again to find which part might answer the question. Circle the key sentences. Read the part(s) of the text(s) you have circled again carefully and choose the one that answers the question. Be careful: a text might use the same words as the question, but not give the right answer. You have to find the text that answers the question using different words.

See the short example below. In this example, David uses the words *action films* but A is not the correct answer. David says *I don't mind action films*, which means he thinks action films are all right, but this is not the same as saying he likes them. B is the correct answer. Michael says *exciting ... cars racing around:* this describes what happens in an action film, but he doesn't actually use the words *action films*.

COMMON MISTAKE: To choose a text because it uses the same words as the question.

YOU SHOULD: Read personal texts in magazines and on the internet as often as you can. This will help you with Part 2, which usually focuses on people talking about themselves.

Three students talk about their favourite film

David

I like comedies most of all. I don't mind action films, but they all seem the same to me ...

Michael

My favourite films are exciting ones – for example, cars racing around, police trying to catch the bad guys ...

John

The best films I've seen are about famous people. I saw a film about President Lincoln once and I learned ...

		David	Michael	John
7	Who likes action films?	A	B	C

Reading Part 3

In this part of the test, you read one longer text in the style of a magazine or newspaper article. Then you have to answer five multiple-choice questions. Here is a (very short) example:

The tallest man in the world
by Joe Norton, 14

We think the tallest man who has ever lived was Robert Wadlow, an American man who was 2.72 metres tall. However, it is not easy to know if Robert really is the tallest man in history. Some people say there were taller people before him, but we can say he is the tallest person whose height we are sure of.

---

14 Robert Wadlow

 A is the tallest living man.

 B is the tallest man in history.

 C is the tallest man we know about.

This part tests your understanding of important ideas and also your understanding of details. First, read the text for general understanding. Then read it again to understand it in detail. Next, read the first question or sentence beginning and find the part of the text that answers or completes it. Circle the key sentences. The questions follow the order of the text, so the answer for the first question will probably be in the first paragraph. Read the questions /sentence beginnings carefully, underline the key words, and check options A–C against the text. Choose the option with the same meaning as the text. As with parts 1 and 2, be careful because the options might use words from the text but mean something different.

In the question above, A says *tallest living man* but we don't know if Robert Wadlow is still living or if he is dead. *Tallest living man* doesn't mean the same as *the tallest man who has ever lived*, so A isn't correct. B isn't correct because the text says *it is not easy to know if Robert really is the tallest man in history*. The correct answer is C. It uses different words from the text – *we know about* – but the meaning is the same as *we are sure of*.

COMMON MISTAKES: To look at the questions before reading the text. / To choose an answer because it uses the same words as the text.

YOU SHOULD: Read the text first and then the questions. Circle the correct part of the text and match it to the option with the same meaning. Read as much English as you can to improve your general reading skills. Do test practice nearer the time of your test, but don't stop developing your general reading skills.

Reading Part 4

In this part of the test, you have to fill in six gaps in a text that gives information on a topic. You are given three words to choose from for each gap and you have to choose the right one.

Here is a short example:

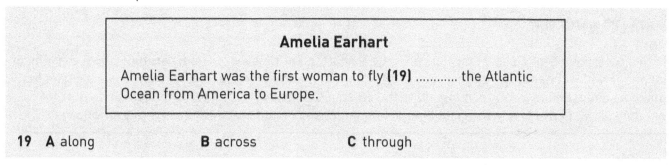

Amelia Earhart

Amelia Earhart was the first woman to fly **(19)** .... the Atlantic Ocean from America to Europe.

19   **A** along   **B** across   **C** through

This part mainly tests your vocabulary. First, read the text to understand its general meaning. Then read the sentence with the gap again carefully and try to choose the correct word to complete it. In the example above, the correct answer is B. If you are not sure, read the sentence with each of the words A–C. This might help you choose the correct one. When you have finished, read the text again to check your answers.

COMMON MISTAKE: To try to fill in the gaps without reading the whole text first.

YOU SHOULD: Read the text for general understanding before you fill in the gaps. When you have finished, read the text again with your answers for a final check.

Reading Part 5

In this part of the test, you have to fill in six gaps in a text with one word in each gap. The text is an email or message that you might write to a friend or someone you know. Here is a short example:

EMAIL	
From:	Frank
To:	Miles

Thank you for your email. I'm sorry It's taken me so long **(25)** .... reply.

This part mainly tests your grammar. First, read the text for general understanding. Then try to think of words to fill in the gaps. The missing words are often small words, like *the, a, is, there, at*, but they could also be longer words. Do the easy gaps first and then try your best with the harder ones. Remember to use only one word and spell it correctly.

In the example above, the correct answer is *to*. The following word, *reply*, is a verb and in this sentence, you need the verb form *to reply*.

COMMON MISTAKE: To try to fill in the gaps without reading the whole text first.

YOU SHOULD: Read the whole text first. With a difficult question, make a list of possible words and choose the best one. Read the text again at the end with your answers for a final check.

Writing Part 6

In this part of the test, you have to write a message (a note or an email) to a friend or someone you know. The situation and the three points you must include are given to you. Here is an example:

You want to invite your friend Jay to come to the cinema with you.
Write an email to Jay.

In your email:
- invite Jay to the cinema
- say what film you want to see
- say where and when you want to meet.

Write **25 words** or more.

In this part, you have to show that you can write a short, clear message. Think carefully about the kind of language you will need, e.g. do you have to offer something to someone (e.g. *Would you like* a cup of tea?), make a suggestion (e.g. *Why don't we* go to the cinema?) or ask someone for their opinion (e.g. *What do you think?*)? You have to use the right kind of language, and include all three points in your answer.

Hi Jay,
Would you like to come to the cinema with me? There's a good comedy on and I think we'd both like it. We could meet on Friday at 6.00 p.m. in front of the cinema.
Karen

This text is a good answer because:
- it uses the right kind of language for inviting someone (*Would you like to …?*) and for making a suggestion (*We could …*)
- it answers all three points
- it is more than 25 words.

COMMON MISTAKE: Not to include one of the points in your answer.

YOU SHOULD: Think about and use the correct kind of language in your answer. When you prepare for your test, revise language for introducing yourself and other people, asking for and giving information, giving advice, agreeing and disagreeing, etc.

Writing Part 7

In this part of the test, you are given three pictures and you have to write a story using every picture. Use words such as *and* and *but* to link sentences. Also try to use words that show the order in which things happen, e.g. *then, next, after that*. It is a good idea to use past tenses and names for the people in your story. See the example on the next page.

Look at the three pictures.
Write the story shown in the pictures.
Write **35 words** or more.

> *One day Neil and Laurence were playing tennis. It was a beautiful sunny day and they were enjoying their game. Then it started to rain and they ran to get out of the rain. After that, they went to the cinema.*

The text above is a good answer because:

- it talks about all the pictures
- it uses a joining word (*and*)
- it uses words that show what happened when (*Then, After that*)
- it uses names (*Neil, Laurence*)
- It uses correct past tenses (e.g. *were playing, started*).

COMMON MISTAKES: To write about only two of the pictures. / To make mistakes with the tenses.

YOU SHOULD: Prepare for the test by writing sentences using past tenses to tell a story.

Listening Part 1

In this part of the test, there are five multiple-choice questions. For each question, you see three pictures, A–C. You will hear two people (occasionally just one person) talking in an everyday situation and you have to choose the correct picture. Here is an example, followed by the recording:

What time is the bus home?

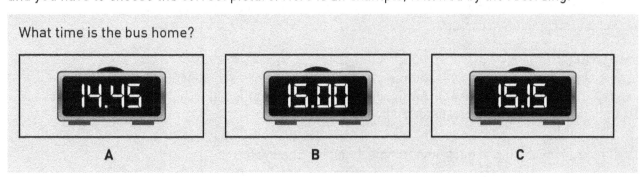

| A | B | C |

Girl: *What time is the bus home? It's at two forty-five, isn't it?*
Boy: *Yes, I think so. Wait. I wrote it down. No, it's three o'clock.*
Girl: *Oh. Is there a bus at quarter past three? There are more things I want to buy.*
Boy: *I don't think so.*

You have five seconds to look at the pictures for a question before you hear the recording. You will hear the recording twice. Be careful: the people might talk about something you see in a picture, but this might not answer the question. The first time you hear the recording, listen for the answer. Check your answer when you hear the recording a second time.

In the recording for the question above, you hear all the times in the pictures, but only B answers the question *What time is the bus home?*

COMMON MISTAKE: Choosing a picture just because you hear words that describe it in the recording.

YOU SHOULD: Look at the pictures carefully and chose the one that answers the question.

Listening Part 2

In this part of the test, there is a set of notes with five gaps. You will hear a person giving information in an everyday or school situation. You have to listen and complete the notes. In each gap, you have to write one word or a number or a date or a time. Here is a short example, followed by the recording:

You will hear a teacher telling students about lunchtime.

Lunchtime	
Lunchtime finishes at:	(6) ....

Teacher: *Now, today we are going to have a short lunchtime because of the football match this afternoon. This means you have to be back here after lunch at 1.15. Don't be late please.*

This part tests if you can listen for detailed information. You have ten seconds before you hear the recording. You will hear the recording twice. Before you listen the first time, use the ten seconds to read the sentence above the notes: this tells you who the speaker is, who they are talking to, and what they are talking about. Also look at the notes and try to guess what kind of information is needed in each gap. If the missing information is a word, try to spell it correctly. If the speaker spells the word, you have to spell it correctly or you won't get a mark. Check your answers when you hear the recording a second time.

The correct answer in the example above is *1.15 p.m.* or *one fifteen*.

COMMON MISTAKE: To wait for the recording to start without reading the notes and trying to guess what will go in the gaps.

YOU SHOULD: Practise listening to and writing numbers, times and dates, and listening to words being spelled out and writing them correctly.

Listening Part 3

In this part of the test, there are five multiple-choice questions. For each question, there are three options, A–C. You will hear two people having an everyday conversation and you have to choose the correct option. Here is an example, followed by the recording:

You will hear Mark talking to his friend Bonnie about his shopping trip.

11   What did Mark buy on his shopping trip?

   A clothes

   B a computer

   C camping equipment

Bonnie: *Hi Mark! How did the shopping go? Did you get everything you wanted?*

Mark: *Not really. When I got to the shopping centre, I saw signs about the sales next week. If I wait until then, I can get discounts on a computer and camping equipment. But I bought some things to wear because I need them now.*

This part tests if you can listen for detailed information. You have 20 seconds to look at the questions before you hear the recording. You will hear the recording twice. Before you listen the first time, use the 20 seconds to read the sentence above the notes: this tells you who the speakers are and what they are speaking about. Also read the five questions or sentence beginnings; this will give you a good idea what to listen for. Be careful: don't choose an option just because it uses the same words as the recording. The correct option might use different words to answer the question. Check your answers when you hear the recording a second time.

The correct answer in the example above is A. You don't hear the word *clothes* in the recording, but you hear *things to wear*, which is another way of talking about clothes.

COMMON MISTAKE: To choose an option just because you read the same words as you hear.

YOU SHOULD: Read the options carefully, listen to the recording, and try to find the answer that has the same meaning as the recording.

Listening Part 4

In this part of the test, there are five multiple-choice questions. For each question, there are three options, A–C. You will hear one or two people talking in an everyday situation and you have to choose the correct option. Here is an example, followed by the recording:

You will hear a girl talking about her journey. How did she travel?

A by plane

B by train

C by coach

Girl: *I'm so tired! It was such a long journey! But at least I had a window seat so I could look at the countryside. It was beautiful, but when we got into town, the traffic was terrible and it was really slow.*

This part tests if you can understand the general meaning of a conversation. You have five seconds to read the question before you hear the recording. You will hear the recording for each question twice. Before you listen the first time, use the ten seconds to read the sentence and question carefully: these tell you who the speakers are, what they are talking about, and what you have to listen for. Don't worry if you can't understand every word in the recording. You will probably understand enough to answer the question. The correct option might use different words from the recording. Check your answers when you hear the recording a second time.

The correct answer in the example above is C. All options have window seats, but only a coach travels on the road and can be caught in traffic.

COMMON MISTAKE: To get worried because the options don't use the same words as the recording.

YOU SHOULD: Read the sentence and question carefully and get ready to listen for the answer to the question.

Listening Part 5

In this part of the test, you have to match five people to five options from a choice of eight. You will hear two people talking about an everyday topic. See the example on the next page. Here's the recording:

Maisy: *We need something to listen to, don't we? So people can dance if they want to.*
Ben: *Helen's always talking about her favourite bands. Let's ask her to take care of that.*

You will hear Maisy and Ben planning a school party. What will the people do for the party?

People		Things to do for the party
21 Helen	☐	**A** bring the cake
22 Jake	☐	**B** prepare the music

This part tests if you can listen for detailed information. You have 15 seconds before you hear the recording. You will hear the recording twice. Before you listen the first time, use the 15 seconds to read the sentence: this tells you who the speakers are and what they are talking about. Also look at the list of things and try to guess what words the speakers might use to talk about them. You have to listen carefully for the name of each person and then listen for something which means the same as one of the options. Be careful: sometimes one of the speakers might give information that isn't correct, and the other speaker corrects them. Check your answers when you hear the recording the second time.

The correct answer for question 21 in the example above is B. Maisy and Ben don't actually use the word *music*; they use *listen to* and *bands*, which show they are talking about music.

COMMON MISTAKE: To choose an option just because you read the same words as you hear.

YOU SHOULD: Get ready to listen by reading the options and thinking about how the speakers might talk about them using different words.

Speaking Part 1
You will have your speaking test with another student, or sometimes with two other students. In this part of the test, you have to answer questions that the examiner asks you. The examiner will ask you your name, your age and where you are from or where you live. Then they will ask you a question about an everyday topic. Here is an example followed by a good answer:

Examiner: *What is your favourite food?*

Student: *My favourite is my mum's pizza that she makes at home. I love it because she puts delicious things on top of it.*

A good answer often has two sentences. The second sentence explains or adds details about the information in the first one. You can find examples of good answers in the **Model answers for Speaking** section at the back of the book.

COMMON MISTAKE: To give a one-word or short one-sentence answer.

YOU SHOULD: Give a two-sentence answer.

Speaking Part 2
In this part of the test, you have to talk about some pictures with the other student and answer questions that the examiner asks you. The pictures allow you to compare things, like different sports or different ways of travelling. You can find examples of good answers for talking about pictures in the **Model answers for Speaking** section at the back of the book. The important thing is to look at the other student and have a conversation with them. Listen to what they say, ask for their opinion, and say if you agree or disagree with them, giving reasons for your answers, e.g. *I don't like travelling by bus because ...*

COMMON MISTAKES: To look only at the examiner and not to listen to the other student. / To give short answers which you don't explain.

YOU SHOULD: Have a real conversation with the other student and smile and show an interest in what they are saying. Practise giving your opinion, giving reasons and asking for someone's opinion.

Test 1

TEST 1 READING AND WRITING

Part 1

Questions 1–6

For each question, choose the correct answer.

1

NOTICE BOARD

The cafeteria will be closed tomorrow for building work. Please bring your own lunch.

A You can eat your own lunch in the cafeteria tomorrow.

B People cannot eat in the cafeteria tomorrow.

C The cafeteria will serve lunch tomorrow.

2

Hi John,

Rebecca wants to join our homework group. She talks in class a lot, so I'm not sure. What do you think?

Mary

What does Mary want John to do?

A talk to Rebecca about their homework

B join a homework group with Rebecca

C give his opinion about Rebecca

3

FOUND

Nearly new trainers in the sports hall on Friday. See Mr Jones.

A Mr Jones has bought some nearly new trainers.

B If you would like a new pair of trainers, see Mr Jones.

C Speak to Mr Jones if you have lost your trainers.

4

To: Parents
From: School Office
Dear parents, The school holiday dates have been changed. Please see the website for details or ask at the office.

A Read the school website for details about the new holiday dates.

B The school office has changed the holiday dates.

C Ask at the office for details of the website.

5

TICKETS

for the school play are only available online. The office does not accept money.

A You can buy tickets for the school play at the office.

B You have to go online if you want to buy tickets for the school play.

C You can watch the school play online if you buy a ticket.

6

To: Parents
From: The Head Teacher
Dear parents, This Friday is non-uniform day. Students can wear their everyday clothes and give money to charity.

A Students don't have to wear their school uniform on Friday.

B Students have to give some money to charity on Friday.

C If students don't give money to charity, they have to wear their school uniform on Friday.

Part 2

Questions 7–13

For each question, choose the correct answer.

		Helen	Marianne	Edwina
7	Who has a pet that another family member does not like?	A	B	C
8	Who does not want her pets to be bored?	A	B	C
9	Whose pet cannot be near another animal in her home?	A	B	C
10	Whose pet has a name that describes its colour?	A	B	C
11	Whose pets are different animals but enjoy being together?	A	B	C
12	Who spends a lot of time looking after her pets?	A	B	C
13	Whose pet eats other small animals?	A	B	C

Three children and their pets

Helen

I have two dogs and a cat. I love them all, but I love my cat the most because she was my first pet. My parents gave her to me when she was tiny. Her name is Snowy because she is white and when we got her it was snowing! Believe it or not, the dogs love Snowy too. They all sleep together under the kitchen table. I love taking the dogs for walks, but Snowy never wants to join us.

Marianne

I keep fish as pets. They are small, colourful and very beautiful. I can't play with them, but I watch them for hours. I feed them twice a day, but I have to be careful not to give them too much to eat. I check the water all the time, clean the tank every month and put new things in the water to make their home interesting for them. My fish all have names and they know who I am.

Edwina

My family and I have lots of unusual pets. The most unusual one is my pet snake, Sid. I play with him every day, but a lot of people are scared of him. My sister won't let him near her and my friends don't want to play with him either. Sid eats mice and insects once a week – we get them for him from the pet shop regularly. My brother has a bird and we make sure that Sid and the bird stay a long way from each other.

Part 3

Questions 14–18

For each question, choose the correct answer.

The world's largest school

by Nyra Anand, 13

It is 7.15 in the morning in Lucknow, India, and thousands of students are starting to arrive at City Montessori School (CMS) to begin their day. With students who range in age from five to seventeen, and with over 7,500 students in one school building, CMS is the largest school in the world.

The students at CMS do not all study in one place. There are classrooms in seventeen different locations in the city. In total, over 55,000 students go to CMS. Almost all of the school's classrooms are full and it is difficult for many parents to get their child a place at the school.

'My parents wanted me to come here for a better education,' says twelve-year-old Ramesh, who is going to start at the school this year. 'I want to become a doctor, so I need very good exam results to get into university. Being at this school will help me do that, and I'll also make lots of friends with different interests. I wouldn't like to study anywhere else.'

When CMS was started in 1959 by Jagdish Gandhi and his wife Bharti, it had five students, all from the same family. The school has grown and changed a lot since then. It is popular because most of its students get excellent exam grades, but getting good marks is not the only important thing. The school also tries to teach its students to be good human beings who will make the world a better place.

---

14 City Montessori School

    A starts at 7.15 in the morning.

    B teaches children from the age of five.

    C has 7,500 pupils in one class.

15 There are

    A many thousands of students at the school.

    B seventeen different classrooms in the school.

    C too many students in the classrooms.

16 Ramesh

    A has made a lot of friends since he started school.

    B knows what he wants to do when he leaves school.

    C says his parents want him to be a doctor one day.

17 The first students at the school in 1959

    A were Jagdish and Bharti Gandhi's children.

    B were five years old.

    C knew each other.

18 At CMS

    A all the students get good grades in exams.

    B students are taught to become good people.

    C most students are popular.

Part 4

Questions 19–24

For each question, choose the correct answer.

The City of Bath

Bath is a city in the south-west of England. It was **(19)** .... by the Romans in about AD 60 because of the hot springs there. The city became very popular in the eighteenth **(20)** .... Many people came to bathe in the warm water that comes from under the ground because they thought it was good **(21)** .... their health. Today, people still come to Bath to bathe in the water. They also come to **(22)** .... the city's many beautiful old buildings. About 400,000 of the visitors to the city are **(23)** .... tourists. This **(24)** .... Bath one of the most visited cities in England.

Nowadays, about 100,000 people live in Bath, which has two universities and is the cultural and economic centre of its region.

---

19 **A** made   **B** done   **C** built

20 **A** date   **B** century   **C** year

21 **A** for   **B** at   **C** with

22 **A** see   **B** watch   **C** look

23 **A** strange   **B** foreign   **C** national

24 **A** means   **B** keeps   **C** makes

Part 5

Questions 25–30

For each question, write the correct answer.
Write **one** word for each gap.

Example: | **0** | *you* |

> **EMAIL**
>
> From: Harry
>
> To: Joey
>
> Hi Joey,
>
> How are **(0)** .... ? I hope you're well. I haven't seen you for a long time! **(25)** .... you have any plans for this weekend? If you don't, **(26)** .... you like to meet? I'm free **(27)** .... Saturday and Sunday. We could go and watch a football game if **(28)** .... weather is nice. But if it's raining, we could do something inside, such **(29)** .... go to the cinema. Just tell **(30)** .... what you want to do. But if you're busy, maybe we could meet next weekend.
>
> Bye!
> Harry

Part 6

Question 31

You made a plan to go shopping with your friend Ellie tomorrow, but now you are sick and you cannot go. Write an email to Ellie.

In your email:
- say you are sorry
- say why you can't go shopping
- suggest another time to go shopping.

Write **25 words** or more.

Write the email on your answer sheet.

Part 7

Question 32

Look at the three pictures.
Write the story shown in the pictures.
Write **35 words** or more.

 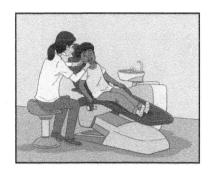 

Write the story on your answer sheet.

TEST 1 LISTENING

Part 1

Questions 1–5

For each question, choose the correct answer.

---

1 What has the boy lost?

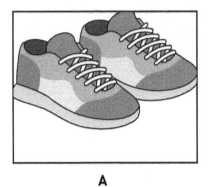

A   B   C

2 What day is football practice?

Tuesday	**Wednesday**	**Thursday**
A	B	C

3 What sport will Jane do at the sports centre?

A   B   C

4   How much money does the boy need to buy tickets for the school play?

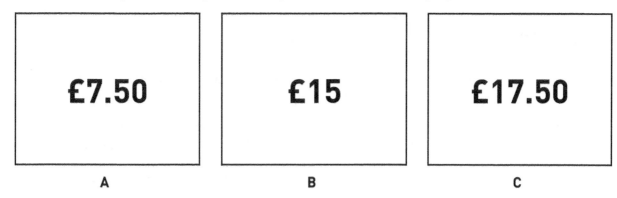

£7.50   £15   £17.50

A   B   C

5   What did the girl see on her school trip?

A   B   C

Part 2

02

Questions 6–10

For each question, write the correct answer in the gap. Write **one word** or **a number** or **a date** or **a time**.

You will hear a teacher giving students information about a visitor who is coming to the school.

Class visitor

A talk about:	a local business
Name of visitor:	Mr **(6)** ....
Type of business:	**(7)** ....
Time of talk:	from 11.15 a.m. to **(8)** .... p.m.
Number of words in project:	**(9)** ....
Hand in date:	Friday **(10)** ....

Part 3

03

Questions 11–15

For each question, choose the correct answer.

You will hear John talking to Monica about his trip to London.

11 In London

    A it was raining.

    B the traffic wasn't a problem.

    C the weather was fine.

12 Somebody stole John's wallet

    A before he got on the train.

    B while he was on the train.

    C as soon as he got to London.

13 John lost

    A some money.

    B some cards.

    C his bank card.

14 The police said

    A John probably won't get his wallet back.

    B John should keep his bank card in his wallet.

    C John should carry only a little cash.

15 In the afternoon

    A nobody knew what to do.

    B John's parents were angry with each other.

    C everybody had different ideas about what to do.

Part 4

04

Questions 16–20

For each question, choose the correct answer.

_____

16 You will hear a teacher talking to a student.
Why is the teacher angry?

    A The student is late for the lesson.

    B The student was chatting.

    C The student hasn't done his homework.

17 You will hear two friends talking.
Where have they been?

    A to a football match

    B to the cinema

    C to the theatre

18 You will hear a girl talking.
Why couldn't she sleep last night?

    A Her neighbours were having a party.

    B She was worried about school.

    C Her dad was angry with her.

19 You will hear two friends planning an activity.
What do they decide to do?

    A go to the swimming pool

    B go to the park

    C go to the beach

20 You will hear a student talking.
What has he lost?

    A his diary

    B his laptop

    C his mobile phone

Part 5

Questions 21–25

For each question, choose the correct answer.

You will hear two teachers talking about parents' evening at school.
What will each student talk about?

Example:

0   Dennis | E |

People

21   Helen   ☐

22   Shazad   ☐

23   Brian   ☐

24   Amal   ☐

25   Mary   ☐

Items

A   maths

B   English

C   history

D   geography

E   science

F   homework

G   school clubs

H   school uniform

You now have six minutes to write your answers on the answer sheet.

TEST 1 SPEAKING

You are Candidate B. Answer the questions.

06–07

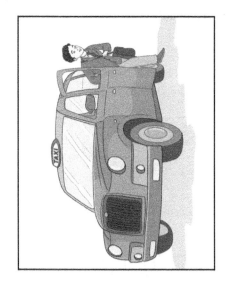

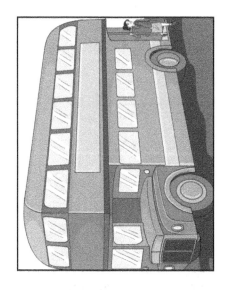

Do you like these different ways of getting to school?

Audio scripts on pages 166–193 and Model answers on pages 205–221.

Test 2

TEST 2 READING AND WRITING

Part 1

Questions 1–6

For each question, choose the correct answer.

1

Dave, we haven't got enough plates for the party. Please get some from Jemma's house. Her mum will be home at six.

Love, Mum

A Mum wants Dave to bring plates for the party.

B Jemma hasn't got enough plates for the party.

C The party will be at Jemma's mum's house at six.

2

NOTICE!
Chess Club won't meet tomorrow because of today's competition. Back to Tuesdays next week.

A The competition has been changed to Tuesday next week.

B There is a chess competition tomorrow.

C Chess Club usually meets on Tuesdays.

3

John, I can't walk to school with you this morning as usual. My mum's ill and I have to take my brother to school.

Ben

A Ben's mum usually takes Ben and John to school.

B Ben usually takes his brother to school.

C Ben's brother can't go to school on his own.

4

To: Parents
From: The Head Teacher
During 'Eat Healthy Week', please give your child one piece of fruit a day to bring to school.
Thank you!

The head teacher wants

A children to bring fruit to school on one day during 'Eat Healthy Week'.

B children to bring fruit to school every day during 'Eat Healthy Week'.

C to give children one piece of fruit every day during 'Eat Healthy Week'.

5

MAFEKING ROAD CLOSED

8–11 July

Please follow signs and use Courtney Street instead.

A You can't use Mafeking Road for four days in July.

B You can use Courtney Street to get to Mafeking Road.

C You cannot use Mafeking Road or Courtney Street from 8–11 July.

6

Lucy, projects need groups of three. Shall we ask Fatima to join us? Can you ask her? Or we might have to have Wanda.

Carrie

A Carrie wants Fatima to work with Wanda.

B Carrie doesn't want to work with Wanda.

C Carrie wants Lucy to work with Wanda.

Part 2

Questions 7–13

For each question, choose the correct answer.

		Malik	Stephen	Brendan
7	Who wears clothes that are different from the clothes most children wear to school?	A	B	C
8	Who doesn't say what colour his uniform is?	A	B	C
9	Who can sometimes take off some of his uniform at school?	A	B	C
10	Who says that parts of his uniform are the all same colour?	A	B	C
11	Who will get into trouble if his uniform is dirty?	A	B	C
12	Who goes to a school where the girls can choose between two things to wear?	A	B	C
13	Who goes to a school where students can all wear different clothes?	A	B	C

Three students talk about the clothes they wear to school

A Malik

The teachers at my school are very strict about what we wear. We have to wear a school jacket, which is black, and a black tie. We wear black trousers and black shoes. If a teacher thinks a student's uniform doesn't look nice and clean, he is sent to the Head Teacher's office, and the Head Teacher gets really angry with students who don't look smart. My school is for boys only. Maybe that's why they're strict about our school uniform!

B Stephen

My school uniform isn't very different from what students wear in most schools. Boys wear a jacket, tie and long trousers. Girls also wear a jacket and tie, but they can wear trousers or skirts. Their skirts can be long, but they can't be shorter than their knees. Our jackets are a nice colour, but they can be uncomfortable sometimes. On hot days the Head Teacher puts a picture of the sun outside her office and then we don't have to wear our jackets and ties.

C Brendan

Our school is unusual because it doesn't have a uniform, but there are still lots of rules about things that students can wear. For example, everybody has to wear proper shoes, not trainers, and short skirts for girls aren't allowed. We also get into trouble if we wear jeans! Boys must wear a shirt and girls must wear a blouse with a collar. Our head teacher says students don't have to look the same, but they have to look smart.

Part 3

Questions 14–18

For each question, choose the correct answer.

How rugby began

by Jamie Colder, 12

Did you know that rugby is played by more than eight million people around the world in more than 120 countries and is becoming more popular every year? The 2019 Rugby World Cup was watched by over 857 million people!

But where did rugby come from? People say that rugby began one day at Rugby School in the town of Rugby in England in 1823 while a group of boys were playing football. In those days, football players were allowed to catch the ball, but they were not allowed to run with it.

The story is that one of the boys, William Webb Ellis, caught the ball during the game, but instead of standing still, he ran forwards with it. He scored a goal by carrying it over the line. The school thought that this made the game better, and the game of rugby was born.

The new game became popular in other boys' schools in England and in other parts of Britain. The first international rugby game was between England and Scotland, and a year later, in 1872, the first of the famous 'Varsity' rugby matches between Oxford and Cambridge took place.

Rugby was played at the Olympic Games for the first time in 1900. However, in 1924 it was dropped from the Olympic programme and didn't return until 2016. Now that it is so popular, it is difficult to imagine the Olympic Games without it.

14 Rugby is

    A played by more than 857 million people every year.

    B played and watched by more and more people every year.

    C the most popular sport in 120 countries around the world.

15 In 1823

    A you could use your hands in a game of football.

    B players could run with the ball in a game of football.

    C football was played in the same way as it is today.

16 William Webb Ellis

    A caught the ball in a new way.

    B scored a goal in an unusual way.

    C wanted to improve the game.

17 The first international game of rugby was played

    A in 1871.

    B in 1873.

    C after the first 'Varsity' match.

18 Rugby

    A has been an Olympic sport since 1900.

    B is not an Olympic sport anymore.

    C is an Olympic sport now.

Part 4

Questions 19–24

For each question, choose the correct answer.

The Blue Whale

Blue whales live in the sea. They are the largest animals that have **(19)** .... lived. They can be **(20)** .... to 30 metres long. The tongue of a blue whale can weigh 2,400 kilogrammes; that's as much as a small elephant. And its heart weighs about 180 kilogrammes; that's as **(21)** .... as an adult lion.

Blue whales eat very small sea animals called krill. They eat by **(22)** .... their mouth with seawater. Then they push the water out of the side of their mouth using their tongue and swallow the krill that are left inside.

Blue whales sometimes swim in groups, but they are usually seen swimming **(23)** .... their own. They often spend the summer in the northern oceans and move to warmer water when winter **(24)** ....

19	**A** already	**B** ever	**C** just
20	**A** in	**B** from	**C** up
21	**A** heavy	**B** thick	**C** thin
22	**A** drinking	**B** filling	**C** putting
23	**A** by	**B** with	**C** on
24	**A** arrives	**B** opens	**C** enters

Part 5

Questions 25–30

For each question, write the correct answer.
Write **one** word for each gap.

Example: | **0** | *Have* |

> **EMAIL**
>
> From: | Ellen
>
> To: | Eva
>
> Hi Eva,
>
> **(0)** .... you done the maths homework yet? You probably have! You always do so well **(25)** .... school. I don't know **(26)** .... to do it and I hope you can help me. I can do the first question, but the other questions **(27)** .... really hard.
> I **(28)** .... listening to the teacher carefully in class, but I didn't understand what she said.
> **(29)** .... you have time to speak to me tonight? If you have time, **(30)** .... time can I call?
>
> Ellen

Part 6

Question 31

Your friend Jay has invited you to lunch at his house tomorrow.
Write an email to Jay.

In your email:

- thank him and say that you will come
- ask for directions to his house
- offer to bring something.

Write **25 words** or more.

Write the email on your answer sheet.

Part 7

Question 32

Look at the three pictures.
Write the story shown in the pictures.
Write **35 words** or more.

Write the story on your answer sheet.

TEST 2 LISTENING

Part 1

Questions 1–5

For each question, choose the correct answer.

___

1 What will the weather be like at the beach?

| A | B | C |

2 What is Sophie going to do with her friend?

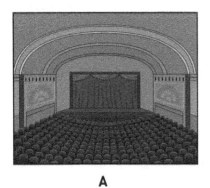

| A | B | C |

3 What is the boy going to read on the train?

| A | B | C |

4 What is the girl going to have at the café?

A

B

C

5 What time will the football game finish?

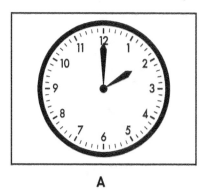

A

B

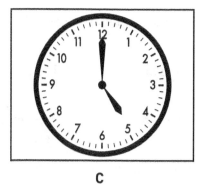

C

Part 2

09

Questions 6–10

For each question, write the correct answer in the gap. Write **one word** or **a number** or **a date** or **a time**.

You will hear a student giving a talk about honey bees in a biology class.

Honey bees

Number of types of honey bee in the world: 8

Number of types of honey bee in the UK: **(6)** ....

Bees important for **(7)** .... and vegetables

Bees save UK **(8)** .... millions of pounds a year

Bees stop flying when the temperature is below: **(9)** .... degrees

Worker bees live from **(10)** .... to 28 days

Part 3

10

Questions 11–15

For each question, choose the correct answer.

You will hear Philippa talking to her friend James about moving house.

11 Philippa's dad

    A lost his job.

    B got a job with another company.

    C is living in the new house.

12 Philippa

    A will be able to walk from her new house to school.

    B will continue to go to the same school.

    C will get a train to school from the city centre.

13 Philippa

    A will share a bedroom with her sister.

    B has her own bedroom at the moment.

    C doesn't like sharing a bedroom with her sister.

14 Philippa says that

    A her parents do not like a lot of noise.

    B her parents would let her have a quiet party.

    C her parents would be happy to have a party.

15 James suggests that

    A Philippa's parents go out instead of having a party.

    B Philippa's parents leave the house during the party.

    C Philippa's parents can stop the party if it is too noisy.

Part 4

11

Questions 16–20

For each question, choose the correct answer.

---

16 You will hear a student talking to a teacher.
    Why didn't she do her homework?

    A She went to the hospital with her sister.

    B She visited her mum in hospital.

    C She visited her sister in hospital.

17 You will hear two friends talking.
    What are they eating?

    A sandwiches

    B pizza

    C burgers

18 You will hear a boy talking about a film he saw.
    What was the film like?

    A It was boring.

    B It was frightening.

    C It was funny.

19 You will hear two friends getting ready to play a game.
    What game are they going to play?

    A tennis

    B football

    C basketball

20 You will hear a girl talking about her pet.
    What sort of animal is it?

    A a cat

    B a dog

    C a rabbit

Part 5

12

Questions 21–25

For each question, choose the correct answer.

___

You will hear two students talking about their group project.
Who will do the different parts of the project?

Example:

0 Oliver | C |

___

People		**Parts of the project**
21 Mia [ ]		**A** write it
22 Lucas [ ]		**B** prepare the cover
23 Mehmet [ ]		**C** print it
24 Jess [ ]		**D** check it
25 Ava [ ]		**E** take the photographs
		F do the maths
		G give the talk
		H draw the poster

You now have six minutes to write your answers on the answer sheet.

Test 2 SPEAKING

You are Candidate B. Answer the questions.

13–14

Do you like these different games?

Audio scripts on pages 166–193 and Model answers on pages 205–221.

Test 3

TEST 3 READING AND WRITING

Part 1

Questions 1–6

For each question, choose the correct answer.

1

HEAD TEACHER

You can only see the head teacher with an appointment.

A You can see the head teacher any time you want to.

B You only need to make an appointment if you want to see the head teacher alone.

C You must make an appointment if you want to see the head teacher.

2

Craig, sorry. I have to see my teacher at lunch-time. I can't change it. Will you tell Matt? Maybe we can meet after school.

Brandon

A Craig can't change his lunchtime meeting with Matt.

B Craig, Matt and Brandon planned a lunchtime meeting.

C Craig can't see his teacher at lunchtime.

3

English language practice

Preparing for an exam?
Want practice speaking English?

Phone Maisy
01964 376394

A Phone Maisy if you want to improve your English.

B Maisy needs help to prepare for an English exam.

C Maisy wants somebody to practise English with her.

4

To: Parents
From: The Head Teacher
Subject: School timetable
Please help children check their timetable daily. Many students arrive in class without the correct books.

The head teacher

A wants parents to check their child's timetable for them.

B wants children to check their timetable every day.

C wants parents to check their child's books for them every day.

5

France Trip Students need to be at least level 3 in French to go.

A If you are level 3 in French, you have to go on the trip.

B If you are level 3 in French, you cannot go on the trip.

C If you are below level 3 in French, you cannot go on the trip.

6

Hi Tracy,

Come and meet me behind the gym. Something terrible has happened. Bring Beth, but don't let Nina hear anything about it.

Zoe

Zoe

A wants to meet Tracy, Beth and Nina.

B says a terrible thing has happened to Nina.

C doesn't want Nina to know something.

Part 2

Questions 7–13

For each question, choose the correct answer.

		Luna	Freya	Elizabeth
7	Who doesn't need to go to bed early?	A	B	C
8	Who plans her studying very carefully?	A	B	C
9	Who shares what she has learned with other students?	A	B	C
10	Who doesn't talk about school work with her friends?	A	B	C
11	Who studies for exams a few weeks before they start?	A	B	C
12	Who doesn't have a problem with exams?	A	B	C
13	Who looks after her health before exams?	A	B	C

Three students talk about preparing for exams

A Luna

I hate exams because I'm always scared I'll get bad marks, but luckily, my friends and I have a study group. A month before the exams, we meet and talk about a subject. Then we divide the subject into smaller parts. We each take one or two parts and go away to work on them. When we meet again, we take turns to talk about what we studied. We really help each other and I don't worry so much.

B Freya

I don't mind exams. When I revise for them, I put up pieces of paper around my desk on my bedroom wall. Then I can easily look at lists and notes about the different topics I have to study. I'm quite happy to stay up late studying and I don't feel tired the next day. I'm lucky because I don't need much sleep. I have great friends and when we get together we have fun, relax and forget about studying.

C Elizabeth

I get very nervous around exam time, but I try to stay calm. I go to bed early and get up early, I take some exercise every day and I eat things like fruit and vegetables. I don't want to get ill! I make myself a study timetable before the exams start so that I know which subject I am going to study every day, and I make sure I follow the timetable. If something happens and I can't follow it, I worry that I won't finish studying.

Part 3

Questions 14–18

For each question, choose the correct answer.

The world's fastest plane

by Janine Foster, 13

The world's fastest passenger plane was Concorde, which was built by the French and the British. It flew for the first time in 1969 and started carrying passengers in 1976. It flew as a passenger plane for 27 years, until 2003.

Concorde travelled at twice the speed of sound. An ordinary plane takes seven or eight hours to fly from London to New York, but Concorde could do the flight in about three hours and 30 minutes. The fastest flight time on a Concorde between these two cities was less than three hours in 1996.

Concorde carried 100 passengers. It flew up to 18,000 metres high and could go 7,200 kilometres without needing to stop. The temperature on the nose of the plane reached 127°C because it was travelling so fast.

Unfortunately, it was very expensive to travel by Concorde. In 1997 it cost $8,000 to fly from London to New York and back, more than 30 times the cost of the cheapest flight. $8,000 in 1997 is the same amount of money as $13,000 in 2019! The plane was also noisy and could only go at full speed over the sea.

In 2000 a Concorde crashed a few minutes after leaving Paris. The plane fell out of the sky and everybody on it died. Concorde stopped flying in 2003 for reasons of cost. The air companies that built and developed Concorde were spending more money on fuel for the plane than they were making from tickets.

---

14 People could pay to travel on Concorde

   A between 1969 and 1976.

   B between 1969 and 2003.

   C between 1976 and 2003.

15 Concorde flew

   A from London to New York in seven or eight hours.

   B at the speed of sound twice.

   C faster than sound.

16 Concorde

   A could take at least 100 passengers.

   B travelled so fast that it was hot inside the plane.

   C didn't fly higher than 18,000 metres.

17 Which statement is true?

   A Concore was very fast, but it was not perfect.

   B A ticket from London to New York on Concorde cost $13,000 in 1997.

   C It cost 30 times more to fly on Concorde than in ordinary planes.

18 Concorde

   A crashed at the airport in Paris.

   B stopped flying because the air companies were losing money.

   C stopped flying when it crashed in Paris.

Part 4

Questions 19–24

For each question, choose the correct answer.

Dartmoor National Park

Dartmoor National Park is a beautiful national park in the southwest of England. It is home to a **(19)** .... of animals, including wild horses, sheep and many kinds of birds. It **(20)** .... a national park in 1951.

Dartmoor has a long history. There are **(21)** .... that people have lived there for thousands of years. It is **(22)** .... possible to see the ruins of homes that were built 3,500 years ago.

Dartmoor is very popular with **(23)** .... and millions of people visit the park every year to see its wildlife and enjoy outdoor activities. These include walking, horse-riding and canoeing. Camping is allowed, but only for one or two nights, and you can only use a small **(24)** ....

19	**A** variety	**B** difference	**C** type
20	**A** started	**B** became	**C** began
21	**A** notices	**B** words	**C** signs
22	**A** still	**B** already	**C** yet
23	**A** guests	**B** visits	**C** tourists
24	**A** roof	**B** tent	**C** address

Part 5

Questions 25–30

For each question, write the correct answer.
Write **one** word for each gap.

Example: | 0 | *are* |

> **EMAIL**
>
> From: Sean
>
> To: Keith
>
> Hi Keith,
>
> How **(0)** .... you? Guess what! We've got a new pet – a dog. I know you have **(25)** .... too, so I'd like to ask you for some advice. **(26)** .... your dog try to eat everything in the house? Our dog never stops! Is **(27)** .... anything we can do about this problem?
>
> We all love our dog very **(28)** .... His name is Matty. He's very friendly and he loves going **(29)** .... walks. You should come and visit us! Our dogs can play together and we can take **(30)** .... to the beach.
>
> Sean

Part 6

Question 31

You want your friend Tanya to help you repair your bike.
Write an email to Tanya.

In your email:

- ask Tanya to help you
- ask her when she can do it
- offer to do something for her.

Write **25 words** or more.

Write the email on your answer sheet.

Part 7

Question 32

Look at the three pictures.
Write the story shown in the pictures.
Write **35 words** or more.

TEST 3 LISTENING

Part 1

Questions 1–5

For each question, choose the correct answer.

___

1   What new clothes does Petra need?

A   B   C

2   What is Marcus going to do after school?

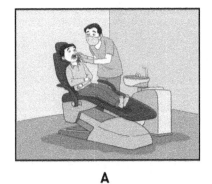

A   B   C

3   When will the girl go on holiday?

JULY	AUGUST	SEPTEMBER
A	B	C

4 Where is the boy's mobile phone?

A

B

C

5 What did the girl have for breakfast?

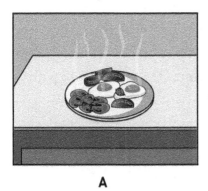

A

B

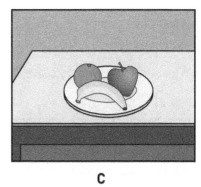

C

Part 2

16

Questions 6–10

For each question, write the correct answer in the gap. Write **one word** or **a number** or **a date** or **a time**.

You will hear a student giving information about school clubs to new students.

School Clubs

How many clubs can students join?	3
What day are sports clubs?	every **(6)** ....
What time are sports clubs?	3–4 p.m. and **(7)** ....–5.15 p.m.
How many students are needed for a club?	**(8)** ....
Who do you contact if want to join the art club?	Mrs **(9)** ....
How much is the music club per term?	**(10)** £...............

Part 3

17

Questions 11–15

For each question, choose the correct answer.

You will hear Henry talking to his friend Charlotte about his grandmother.

11 Henry is going

    A to the hospital.

    B to his aunt's house.

    C to his grandmother's house.

12 Henry wanted to give his grandmother

    A some chocolate.

    B some fruit.

    C some flowers.

13 Henry's grandmother lives

    A in another town.

    B in a ground floor flat.

    C in an upstairs flat.

14 Henry's grandmother

    A lives with her brothers and sisters.

    B had three brothers and four sisters.

    C came from a big family.

15 Henry says that

    A big families were unusual when his grandmother was a child.

    B people do not spend a lot of money on children these days.

    C in the past, children often earned money for the family.

Part 4

18

Questions 16–20

For each question, choose the correct answer.

___

16 You will hear a boy talking about his part-time job.
Where does he work?

   A   in a shop

   B   in a museum

   C   in a library

17 You will hear two girls talking about a new piece of furniture.
What is the piece of furniture?

   A   a sofa

   B   a table

   C   an armchair

18 You will hear a boy talking about an accident he had.
What has he hurt?

   A   his hand

   B   his foot

   C   his head

19 You will hear two teachers talking about an activity.
What activity are they talking about?

   A   painting

   B   dancing

   C   singing

20 You will hear a girl who is unhappy with her food in a restaurant.
What is the problem?

   A   It is too hot.

   B   It does not taste good.

   C   It is too cold.

Part 5

19

Questions 21–25

For each question, choose the correct answer.

You will hear two parents talking about tidying the house.
Which part of the house will each child tidy?

Example:

0   Amy | **G** |

Children

21   Roger   ☐

22   Ruth   ☐

23   Fiona   ☐

24   Chris   ☐

25   Ken   ☐

Parts of the house

A   kitchen

B   bathroom

C   living room

D   bedroom

E   garden

F   dining room

G   garage

H   hall

You now have six minutes to write your answers on the answer sheet.

Test 3 SPEAKING

You are Candidate B. Answer the questions.

20–21

Do you like these different places to eat?

Audio scripts on pages 166–193 and Model answers on pages 205–221.

Test 4

TEST 4 READING AND WRITING

Part 1

Questions 1–6

For each question, choose the correct answer.

1

> **To:** Parents
>
> **From**: Head Teacher
>
> Dear parents,
> Please tell the office if you are coming to Mr Brown's leaving party on Thursday at 4 p.m.

A If parents aren't going to the party, they should tell the office.

B Mr Brown will leave the party on Thursday at 4 p.m.

C Mr Brown will stop working at the school.

2

> **These are self-clear tables!**
>
> **Please clean your table after finishing your meal.**

A You can't eat until you clean your table.

B Clean your table yourself.

C Be careful. The tables are dirty.

3

> Hi Joe,
>
> Can you get more eggs when you go to the supermarket? Sam made a cake and used them all. Thanks.
>
> Mum

A Mum wants to know if Joe needs more eggs.

B Joe is going shopping.

C Sam needs more eggs for a cake.

4

> **To:** School Office
> **From:** Jason Turner
> **Subject:** Mark Turner
>
> Please note that Mark will miss morning classes because of a visit to the dentist.

A Mark will be at school in the afternoon.

B The dentist will visit the school in the morning.

C Mark will be in class in the morning and then go to the dentist.

5

> **MUSIC SCHOOL OPEN DAY!**
>
> **Advice available inside for students interested in playing any instrument.**

A Please give advice if you can play a musical instrument.

B If you want to learn a musical instrument, come inside.

C Students can play their instruments inside.

6

> Mum, can I go home with Tabitha? I know I have a lot of homework, but she has too. We can do it together.
>
> Claire

A Claire and Tabitha both have homework to do.

B Claire wants Tabitha to come home with her after school.

C Claire knows a lot and can help Tabitha with her homework.

Part 2

Questions 7–13

For each question, choose the correct answer.

		Leonard	Kelvin	Bobby
7	Who might get wet on the way to school?	A	B	C
8	Whose parents do not help him get to school?	A	B	C
9	Who has the easiest journey to school?	A	B	C
10	Who can travel to and from school any time he wants to?	A	B	C
11	Who usually needs two forms of transport to get to school?	A	B	C
12	Who has a problem if he has to stay late at school?	A	B	C
13	Who could go to a school that is closer to his home?	A	B	C

Three journeys to school

A Leonard

I live miles from my school, on a farm. Most days, my mum or dad drives me to the train station and I get the train which takes me to school. I don't mind the journey in the summer when the weather is pleasant, but in the winter it can be hard if there's a lot of snow and ice on the road. It's difficult when I have activities after school because there aren't many trains to get back home.

B Kelvin

I have a long journey to school because my home is in a different town from my school. My parents didn't like the local school and they wanted me to attend a better one. It's a nice journey because my mum gives me a lift. I don't have to worry about things like catching a bus or bad weather. Mum works near the school and she can usually stay at the office longer if I want her to pick me up a bit later.

C Bobby

My journey to school is unusual because I go by boat. I live on a small island that isn't big enough to have a local school, so I go to school on a bigger island that's a fifteen-minute boat ride away. Most of the time it's fine, but when the weather is bad, it's not so good – you have to be careful of the water coming over the side of the boat. But at least there are lots of boats that go between the islands.

Part 3

Questions 14–18

For each question, choose the correct answer.

A very strange job

by William Brown, 12

There are few people in the world with the same job as Todd. He is a golf ball diver. He dives into ponds around golf courses and finds golf balls that have been hit into them. Golf balls don't get damaged under water and people buy them from Todd because they are cheaper than new ones.

Todd says people laugh when he tells them what his job is. 'It's a serious job, like any other job. But I can see why people are surprised when I tell them what I do, and I don't mind if they laugh. I've always got something to talk about at parties!'

Todd works at a number of golf courses. He pays them and they let him dive into the water and keep the balls he finds. The average golf course has between four and twelve ponds and Todd spends eight to ten hours a day finding balls.

'You have to wear the correct diving equipment to breathe because some of the ponds are deep and you spend a lot of time underwater. The water is usually black, so you can't see anything, and you have to feel for the balls with your hands,' says Todd.

If you want to be a golf ball diver, you must pass a diving test and to do this, you need 200 hours of diving experience. 'It's not an easy job,' says Todd, 'but if you like being outside and being your own boss, it might the perfect one for you.'

14 The golf balls that Todd sells

    A are a little damaged.

    B cost as much as new ones.

    C were lost by golf players.

15 Todd

    A is happy to talk about his job.

    B does not like it when people laugh at his job.

    C gets bored talking about his job.

16 Todd

    A is paid by golf courses to pick up golf balls.

    B dives for at least eight hours a day.

    C dives into between four and twelve ponds a day.

17 You

    A must have good eyes to be a golf ball diver.

    B need diving equipment to find golf balls in ponds.

    C cannot find golf balls if the water in the pond is black.

18 Golf ball divers must

    A learn to dive when they get the job.

    B like having a boss.

    C have diving experience.

Part 4

Questions 19–24

For each question, choose the correct answer.

Marcus Rashford

Marcus Rashford is a footballer. He started playing with Manchester United at the **(19)** .... of seven. He played for Manchester United's first **(20)** .... when he was only eighteen. He scored twice the first time he played for Manchester United and once the first time he played for England.

Marcus grew up in Manchester. His mother was a single parent who worked hard to **(21)** .... money for her family. She had to do more than one **(22)** .... , so she was often tired. As a young boy, Marcus found it difficult to **(23)** .... to football games on time, but everybody could see how good he was.

Marcus is a rich man today, but he thinks about other people too. He wants to help poor people who don't have **(24)** .... to eat.

19	**A** age	**B** year	**C** date
20	**A** group	**B** club	**C** team
21	**A** earn	**B** bring	**C** win
22	**A** work	**B** job	**C** career
23	**A** get	**B** arrive	**C** be
24	**A** more	**B** less	**C** enough

Part 5

Questions 25–30

For each question, write the correct answer.
Write **one** word for each gap.

Example: | 0 | *for* |

> **EMAIL**
>
> From: Ruby
>
> To: Cora
>
> Hi Cora,
>
> Thanks **(0)** .... your email. I can't believe it's six
> weeks **(25)** .... we moved to our new flat. I miss
> you all so much. **(26)** .... anybody nice moved
> into our old flat? I hope you **(27)** .... friendly
> neighbours! We've met our neighbours here. They're
> a family **(28)** .... us – a mother and a father and
> two girls.
>
> Our flat has lovely views of **(29)** .... sea. You must
> come and visit us soon. You'd love **(30)** .... here!
>
> Ruby

Part 6

Question 31

You forgot to bring your lunch money to school. You want to borrow some money from your friend Alex. Write a note to Alex.

In your note:

- explain your problem to Alex
- ask if you can borrow some money from him
- say when you will give back the money.

Write **25 words** or more.

Write the note on your answer sheet.

Part 7

Question 32

Look at the three pictures.
Write the story shown in the pictures.
Write **35 words** or more.

TEST 4 LISTENING

Part 1

Questions 1–5

For each question, choose the correct answer.

---

1 What time does school start today?

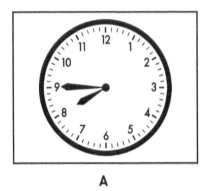

A

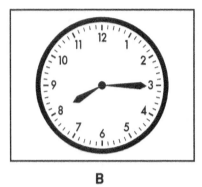

B

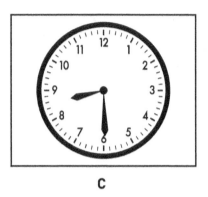

C

2 How is Flora going to talk to her grandmother?

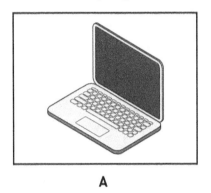

A

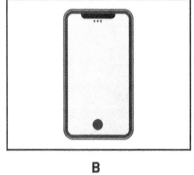

B

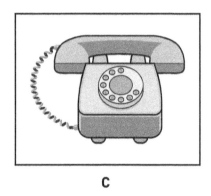

C

3 Where does the girl want to stay?

A

B

C

4 What is Richard going to do after school?

A

B

C

5 How much do the clothes cost?

£66	£60	£16
A	B	C

Part 2

23

Questions 6–10

For each question, write the correct answer in the gap. Write **one word** or **a number** or **a date** or **a time**.

You will hear a teacher telling students about the new school library.

New School Library

The library will be open from:	Monday
The library will open daily at:	**(6)** ....
The new teacher needs help during:	**(7)** ....
If you want to help at the library, see:	Mr **(8)** ....
Students can do their homework:	on the **(9)** .... floor
The opening ceremony is for students and	**(10)** ....

Part 3

24

Questions 11–15

For each question, choose the correct answer.

You will hear Astrid talking to Albert about her new summer job.

11 Astrid

    A is going to start her job on Saturday.

    B has to start her job early.

    C is not sure if she likes her job yet.

12 What is Astrid learning at work?

    A how to clean up and throw old flowers away

    B the difference between fresh and old flowers

    C how to talk to customers about flowers

13 The other people who work in the shop

    A want to enjoy themselves at work.

    B are Mrs Jones's friends.

    C are all sisters.

14 Astrid

    A has to work every Saturday.

    B does not have to work every Saturday.

    C can easily change her work days when she wants to.

15 Astrid thinks that

    A she might come to the beach next Saturday.

    B she will come to the beach next Saturday.

    C she will not come to the beach next Saturday.

Part 4

25

Questions 16–20

For each question, choose the correct answer.

---

16 You will hear two friends talking.
Why are they unhappy?

    A Their team played badly.

    B Their team lost the game.

    C The other team played well.

17 You will hear a brother and sister talking.
How is one of them going to travel?

    A by plane

    B by train

    C by coach

18 You will hear a boy talking about his day.
Where did he go?

    A to the beach

    B to the zoo

    C to the swimming pool

19 You will hear a girl talking.
What has she done?

    A She has had her hair cut.

    B She has had her photograph taken.

    C She has bought some new clothes.

20 You will hear a boy talking to his father about a camping trip.
How long does he want to stay at the campsite?

    A four nights

    B five nights

    C six nights

Part 5

26

Questions 21–25

For each question, choose the correct answer.

You will hear two students talking about photographs for a school project.
Who found the photographs of the animals?

Example:

0 Dennis | E |

People

21 Elaine [ ]

22 Lucas [ ]

23 Mark [ ]

24 Layla [ ]

25 Karen [ ]

Animals

A camel

B rabbit

C tiger

D whale

E bear

F monkey

G lion

H dolphin

You now have six minutes to write your answers on the answer sheet.

Test 4 SPEAKING

You are Candidate B. Answer the questions.

27–28

Do you like these different school clubs?

Audio scripts on pages 166–193 and Model answers on pages 205–221.

Test 5

TEST 5 READING AND WRITING

Part 1

Questions 1–6

For each question, choose the correct answer.

1

SCHOOL OPEN DAY

Please be polite and
helpful to visitors to
our school.

A Visitors to the school should be polite and helpful.

B Students should be friendly to people visiting the school.

C The school is open to polite and helpful vistors.

2

Martin,

Daisy's ill! Shall
we give our class
talk anyway? Or
wait until next
week? I'd just
like it to be
finished.

Jane

Jane would prefer

A to give the talk without Daisy.

B to wait until next week to give the talk.

C Martin to give the talk on his own.

3

| To: Parents |
| From: School Office |
| Subject: Mobile phones |

Dear parents,
Any phones that ring in class
will be collected and given to
the head teacher.

A A student will have to see the head teacher if their phone rings in class.

B Parents should phone the head teacher if they want to speak to their child during lessons.

C The teacher will collect all students' phones before a lesson.

4

Katy,

Shall we talk about our geography project during lunch? Or have you planned something? Hannah can join us.

Ursula

A Ursula wants to meet Katy and Hannah after lunch.

B Ursula wants to talk to Katy and Hannah about their geography project.

C Ursula wants Katy to meet Hannah.

5

Please leave this room as you found it!

Tidy up!

Turn off the lights!

A Students should leave this room immediately.

B Students must turn off the lights and clean the room after using it.

C Students must leave the room if it is not tidy and the lights are not turned off.

6

To: Brian

From: Madelaine

Subject: History teams

Hi Brian,

We're three so far. Would you like to join me, Larry and Donna?

Madelaine

A Madelaine wants Brian to make a team of three with Larry and Donna.

B Madelaine is suggesting two teams: Madelaine with Brian, and Larry with Donna.

C Madelaine wants a team of four.

Part 2

Questions 7–13

For each question, choose the correct answer.

		Parvati	Violet	Juliette
7	Who never knew one of her grandparents?	A	B	C
8	Who asks her grandparents for advice?	A	B	C
9	Whose grandparent had a difficult life?	A	B	C
10	Who spent a lot of time with her grandparents when she was very young?	A	B	C
11	Whose grandparent makes her laugh?	A	B	C
12	Whose grandparent worked in a restaurant?	A	B	C
13	Who is learning useful skills from one of her grandparents?	A	B	C

Three students talk about their grandparents

A   Parvati

In our culture, nothing is more important than family. We respect older people, so the older members of my family are really special. My grandparents have a lot of experience, so if I don't know what to do, I go to them and they always have some good ideas. My mum's mum is a brilliant cook and she also makes all her own clothes. She's teaching me what she knows, so I can make some delicious dishes and beautiful things to wear.

B Violet

My mum's dad died when mum was still a young girl, and Granny had to work very hard to bring up my mum and her sisters without any support from anybody else. Now she lives next door to us and my mum says it's our turn to look after her. My dad's parents live close to us and we see them all the time, at least once a week. My grandad is great fun – he's the funniest person I know. Even my friends love him!

C Juliette

My dad is British and my mum is French and we live in London. That means I don't see my French grandparents very much, unfortunately. But I love visiting them in Paris. Granny was a successful chef and cooks lovely French food. I see my British relatives a lot, including my dad's parents. They often looked after me when I was little, so I know them really well and I'm very close to them.

Part 3

Questions 14–18

For each question, choose the correct answer.

School of the Air

by Bridget Bailey, 13

If you live in a village, you probably think it's a long way to get to town, but imagine living 600 kilometres from your nearest school. However, that's not a problem for Mark because he's a student at the School of the Air. This school was set up to help children like Mark who can't get to school every day.

Mark, aged ten, lives on a farm in a remote part of Australia. He gets up early, but unlike most children, who start the day by going to school, he does jobs around the farm. Then he goes back to the house for breakfast and then he has lessons.

Mark goes to the study, turns on the laptop and meets his teacher online with other students who can't meet face to face. Mark has twelve lessons every week. After his lessons, he works on his projects.

Mark's mother also helps him, making sure he studies at least six hours a day. A teacher visits him once a month to check if he has problems with his lessons. She brings books and learning materials with her. Once a year, Mark and his classmates meet together in a real school for a week with their teacher.

When the School of the Air started in 1951, children sent their homework to their teacher by post. But technology has changed things, and students can now send their homework by email and get it back from their teacher quickly.

14 The School of the Air

    A is 600 kilometres away from Mark's house.

    B is for children who live a long way from schools.

    C helps children to get to school every day.

15 Mark

    A starts the day by going to school.

    B does farm work at the beginning of the day.

    C has a lesson before having breakfast.

16 Students at the School of the Air

    A have lessons online.

    B meet face to face every day.

    C have twelve lessons a week.

17 Mark's

    A mother helps him for six hours every day.

    B teacher visits him to see if he has any problems studying.

    C classmates meet their teacher once a month.

18 Modern technology means that

    A children can hand in their homework late.

    B children can finish their homework more quickly than in the past.

    C children don't have to send their homework to their teacher by post.

Part 4

Questions 19–24

For each question, choose the correct answer.

Mount Everest

Mount Everest is the world's highest mountain. It is 8,848.86 metres high. The first people to **(19)** .... Mount Everest were Tenzing Norgay and Edmund Hillary in 1953. Hillary was from New Zealand and Norgay came from the **(20)** .... area in Nepal. The two men were **(21)** .... of a big team trying to reach the top of the mountain.

These days it is easier to get to the top of Mount Everest. But it still **(22)** .... two months to get there and it is still a dangerous thing to do. Bad weather can **(23)** .... you and worse things can happen. Some people lose their lives when they try. Over 300 people have **(24)** .... on Everest and many of those people's bodies are still on the mountain.

19	**A** walk	**B** run	**C** climb
20	**A** local	**B** close	**C** near
21	**A** people	**B** members	**C** pieces
22	**A** lasts	**B** takes	**C** uses
23	**A** hold	**B** keep	**C** delay
24	**A** died	**B** ended	**C** finished

Part 5

Questions 25–30

For each question, write the correct answer.
Write **one** word for each gap.

Example: | **0** | *about* |

> **EMAIL**
>
> From: Ash
>
> To: Frankie
>
> Hi Frankie,
>
> I hope you're well. I'm emailing you **(0)** .... the
> football match against the kids from Lyttleton village
> this weekend. Can you play **(25)** .... Saturday?
> If you can't play, then I think **(26)** .... won't be
> enough players. Ginger and Dekka have already told
> me **(27)** .... can't. So I might need **(28)** ....
> change the date for the match. If you say yes, you must
> **(29)** .... sure! Please don't say yes and then tell
> **(30)** .... later that you can't come!
>
> Ash

Part 6

Question 31

You want to invite your friend Natalie to a party in the park this weekend.
Write an email to Natalie.

In your email:
- invite Natalie to the party
- say where and when the party is
- suggest what she can bring to the party.

Write **25 words** or more.

Write the email on your answer sheet.

Part 7

Question 32

Look at the three pictures.
Write the story shown in the pictures.
Write **35 words** or more.

TEST 5 LISTENING

Part 1

Questions 1–5

For each question, choose the correct answer.

---

1   What is the girl going to buy?

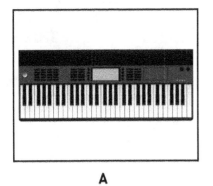

A

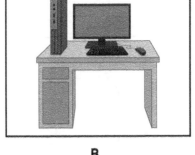

B

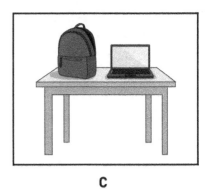

C

2   Where does Joe live?

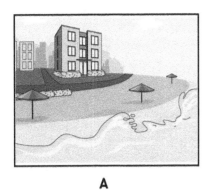

A

B

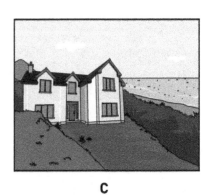

C

3   What did Susan eat?

A

B

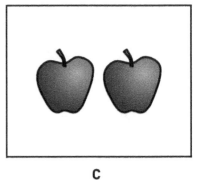

C

4 What is the girl going to wear to the party?

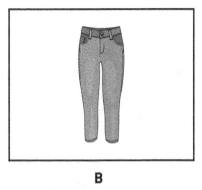

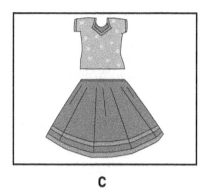

A   B   C

5 How did Kenji get to the hospital?

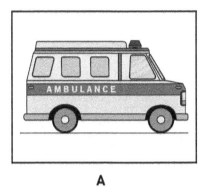

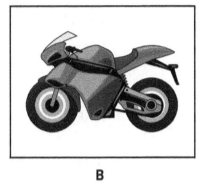

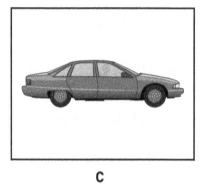

A   B   C

Part 2

30

Questions 6–10

For each question, write the correct answer in the gap. Write **one word** or **a number** or **a date** or **a time**.

You will hear a teacher talking about Sports Day.

Sports Day

Sports Day is on:	Friday
In the morning, go to:	the **(6)** ....
Sports Day begins at:	**(7)** ....
There will be a talk by:	Mr Ben **(8)** ....
All students should take part in:	the **(9)** .... race
Money the school wants to make:	**(10)** £...............

Part 3

31

Questions 11–15

For each question, choose the correct answer.

You will hear Charlie talking to Stephanie about his holiday.

11 Charlie likes to see animals

    A where he lives.

    B outside a zoo.

    C in a zoo.

12 Where did Charlie stay on holiday?

    A He stayed in a tent for most of the time.

    B He stayed in a quiet hotel.

    C He stayed in a tent and in a hotel.

13 Charlie

    A spent too long in the sun.

    B wore things to keep the sun off him.

    C stayed inside during the hot part of the day.

14 What does Charlie say about the food?

    A He wanted to have more vegetables.

    B He didn't like the meat.

    C He didn't eat much.

15 What does Stephanie say about her holiday?

    A The weather was not as good as they hoped it would be.

    B Their hotel was quite noisy at night.

    C The weather and the hotel were not very nice.

Part 4

Questions 16–20

For each question, choose the correct answer.

___

16 You will hear a girl talking to her friend.
Why is she going home?

    A She is tired.

    B She is feeling ill.

    C She has to finish her project.

17 You will hear a girl in a restaurant.
What will she have to eat?

    A chicken and chips

    B chicken and salad

    C chicken without chips and salad

18 You will hear a boy talking about something he did.
Where did he go?

    A to see a band

    B to the cinema

    C to the theatre

19 You will hear a girl talking to a friend.
What has she bought?

    A a mobile phone

    B a laptop

    C a camera

20 You will hear a boy describing an accident.
What has he hurt?

    A his foot

    B his arm

    C his hand

Part 5

33

Questions 21–25

For each question, choose the correct answer.

You will hear a brother and sister talking about family members who are coming to visit.
How will each person travel?

Example:

0   Aunt Edna $\boxed{F}$

People		Ways to travel
21 Erin ☐		**A** by car
22 Harry ☐		**B** on foot
23 Uncle Tony ☐		**C** by coach
24 Fred ☐		**D** by train
25 Aunt Amy ☐		**E** by plane
		F by taxi
		G by bus
		H by bicycle

You now have six minutes to write your answers on the answer sheet.

Test 5 SPEAKING

You are Candidate B. Answer the questions.

34–35

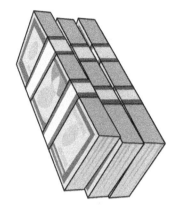

Do you like these different presents for people who have just got married?

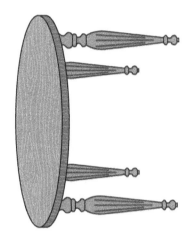

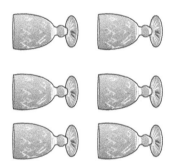

Audio scripts on pages 166–193 and Model answers on pages 205–221.

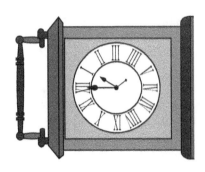

Test 6

TEST 6 READING AND WRITING

Part 1

Questions 1–6

For each question, choose the correct answer.

1

| To: Mr and Mrs Brown |
| From: Head Teacher |
| Subject: Martin |

Please make an appointment with my secretary to speak to me about Martin.

The head teacher

A wants to speak to Mr and Mrs Brown.

B wants to the secretary to speak to Martin.

C wants Mr and Mrs Brown to speak to Martin.

2

Gym shoes ONLY in the hall.
Other shoes leave marks on the floor!

A You can wear gym shoes in the hall, but nowhere else.

B Leave your gym shoes in the hall.

C You must not go into the gym if you are not wearing gym shoes.

3

Jay,

Please bring some stamps and envelopes home with you. But if you're too busy, that's fine. There's no need to let me know.

Mum

A Mum thinks Jay is too busy to get stamps and envelopes.

B It does not matter if Jay cannot get stamps and envelopes.

C Mum wants to know if Jay has time to buy stamps and envelopes.

4

Maisy,

Geoff says 4 is no good. He's suggesting 4.30, but that isn't good for me. Can you do 3.30?

Roger

A Roger can meet at 4 or 4.30.

B Geoff cannot meet at 4.30.

C Roger wants to meet Maisy and Geoff at 3.30.

5

Parents Evening Help needed!
Please speak to Mrs Flood.

Thanks!

A Mrs Flood wants to thank people who helped at Parents Evening.

B Speak to Mrs Flood if you need help at Parents Evening.

C If you can help at Parents Evening, speak to Mrs Flood.

6

Hi Peter,

I fell off my bike and I've hurt my hand. I can't take notes! Can I see yours after class?

Belinda

A Belinda wants to speak to Peter after class.

B Belinda wants something from Peter.

C Belinda cannot take notes for Peter.

Part 2

Questions 7–13

For each question, choose the correct answer.

		Darsh	Jiang	Marcus
7	Whose neighbour tells him not to do things?	A	B	C
8	Who helps his neighbour?	A	B	C
9	Who can visit his neighbours without going through their front door?	A	B	C
10	Whose neighbour lives alone?	A	B	C
11	Who spends a lot of time at their neighbours' home?	A	B	C
12	Whose neighbours are unhappy when it is not quiet?	A	B	C
13	Who would like to have neighbours his age?	A	B	C

Three students talk about their neighbours

A Darsh

My neighbours are great. We've lived next door to them all my life. There are two boys in their family, nearly the same age as my brother and me. Our gardens are next to each other and we can easily jump over the wall to visit each other. Our parents never know whose house we're in! They're our closest neighbours. We have other neighbours too, but we hardly ever see them.

B Jiang

My neighbour is 78 years old and his wife died a few years ago. He doesn't have any other family and I think he's unhappy. We check on him sometimes to see that he's all right. It snowed recently, so I went to his house and asked him if he needed anything from the shops –he'd find it difficult to go out. He's the only neighbour we have. I think it would be nice to have neighbours that I can play with as I live a long way from my friends.

C Marcus

We don't get on with our neighbours. They don't like us to make any noise. When we had a party one night, their dad came to the door and said that we should stop playing music and that everybody should go home – and it was only nine o'clock! He also says we shouldn't kick the football against the garden wall. It would be nice to have friendly neighbours, but as my dad says, you can't choose who you live next to!

Part 3

Questions 14–18

For each question, choose the correct answer.

A very famous ship

by Rhys Hughes, 13

The Queen Elizabeth II (known as the QE2) is one of the most famous ships in the world. It was built for the travel company Cunard as a passenger ship to sail across the Atlantic Ocean between the UK and the USA. It was designed in the company's offices in Southampton and Liverpool, but it was built in Scotland.

The QE2 first went to sea in 1967, but it had some problems. Its first journey across the Atlantic was planned for January 1969, but it was delayed and it couldn't start until May, four months later.

The QE2 could carry 1,892 passengers, and 1,042 people worked on it. It also had five restaurants, two cafés and three swimming pools. It regularly sailed from Southampton to New York, and the fastest time it made the journey was three days, 20 hours and 42 minutes.

The QE2 was also used as a cruise ship for people who wanted a luxury holiday. It sailed to many different places around the world. In 1976, during a trip across the Atlantic Ocean, a fire started on the ship and it had to return to Southampton.

In 2007 the QE2 stopped working as a passenger ship. Cunard sold it to a Dubai company for $100 million and it is now a floating hotel in Dubai. If you stay on the QE2 hotel, you can have a guided tour of the ship and visit its museum, where you can learn about the history of this famous ship.

---

14 The QE2

    A is the most famous ship in the world.

    B was built in the UK and the USA.

    C belonged to the Cunard travel company.

15 The QE2's first journey across the Atlantic

    A took place four months later than planned.

    B took four months to plan.

    C was delayed until January 1969.

16 The QE2

    A carried fewer passengers than workers.

    B had more swimming pools than restaurants.

    C travelled from Southampton to New York in less than four days.

17 In 1976

    A a fire stopped the ship from sailing across the Atlantic.

    B there was a fire when the ship was returning to Southampton.

    C there was a fire in Southampton.

18 Now you can

    A take a guided tour of the ship without staying on it.

    B stay on the QE2 if you visit Dubai.

    C take a cruise on the QE2 from Dubai.

Part 4

Questions 19–24

For each question, choose the correct answer.

Serena Williams

Serena Williams is a professional tennis player. She has often been the number 1 women's tennis player in the world. She was the number 1 player for 186 weeks **(19)** .... February 2013 and September 2016. There are four important tennis **(20)** .... in the world: the US Open, the Australian Open, the French Open and Wimbledon. Serena has won these 23 times.

Serena started playing tennis when she was four. Her parents didn't **(21)** .... her to school. Instead, her father **(22)** .... her at home himself. He also helped her with her tennis.

Serena's sister, Venus, is also a **(23)** .... tennis player. The sisters sometimes play together as a pair and they have won the US Open, the Australian Open, the French Open and Wimbledon many **(24)** ....

---

19   **A** in   **B** from   **C** between

20   **A** matches   **B** competitions   **C** games

21   **A** send   **B** make   **C** push

22   **A** learned   **B** showed   **C** taught

23   **A** careful   **B** successful   **C** interested

24   **A** times   **B** dates   **C** days

Part 5

Questions 25–30

For each question, write the correct answer.
Write **one** word for each gap.

Example: | **0** | *are* |

> **EMAIL**
>
> From: Amy
>
> To: Frieda
>
> Hi Frieda,
>
> I hope you **(0)** .... well. Can you help me? I'd like to ask you for **(25)** .... information. Caroline tells me that you've started taking piano lessons. I'm also looking for a piano teacher. **(26)** .... yours good? I want somebody **(27)** .... is kind. My sister had a piano teacher before, **(28)** .... he got angry when she made mistakes and he shouted at her. I don't want **(29)** .... have a teacher like that! Please tell me if you think I'd enjoy piano lessons **(30)** .... your teacher.
>
> Amy

Part 6

Question 31

Your friend Marlon goes to school by car. You want a lift to school tomorrow because you have a lot of heavy books to carry.
Write an email to Marlon.

In your email:

- ask him for a lift

- explain why you want a lift

- say where and when you will wait for him and his mother.

Write **25 words** or more.

Write the email on your answer sheet.

Part 7

Question 32

Look at the three pictures.
Write the story shown in the pictures.
Write **35 words** or more.

Write the story on your answer sheet.

TEST 6 LISTENING

Part 1

Questions 1–5

For each question, choose the correct answer.

---

1   Who is Uncle Frank?

A

B

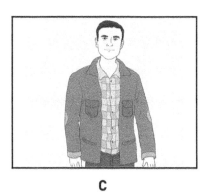

C

2   What time will the girl's father give her a lift home?

A

B

C

3   What job is Jason doing this summer?

A

B

C

4   Which dog is Michael's?

A

B

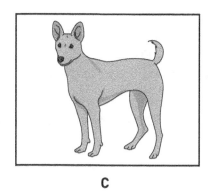
C

5   Where does Mary want to put the food for the party?

A

B

C

Part 2

37

Questions 6–10

For each question, write the correct answer in the gap. Write **one word** or **a number** or **a date** or **a time**.

You will hear a teacher talking about the school play.

School Play

Name of the play:	*A Happy House*
If you want to be in the play, email:	Mrs **(6)** ....
The play will be in a:	**(7)** .... in the city centre
Number of seats available:	**(8)** ....
Adult tickets cost:	**(9)** £...............
Date of the play:	**(10)** ....

Part 3

38

Questions 11–15

For each question, choose the correct answer.

___

You will hear Amna talking to Farhan about a concert.

11 Amna says that

    A the concert wasn't as good as she thought it would be.

    B she and Yasmin are fans of the band.

    C going to the concert wasn't her idea.

12 Amna and Yasmin

    A sat in front of some tall boys.

    B changed their seats to get a better view.

    C couldn't see much at the end of the concert.

13 Amna says that

    A the music was so loud that she couldn't talk to anybody.

    B the songs were too loud.

    C she enjoyed the music.

14 After the concert, Amna and Yasmin went home

    A by train.

    B by bus.

    C by taxi.

15 Farhan

    A doesn't like pop music.

    B doesn't like going to concerts.

    C doesn't like rock music.

Part 4

Questions 16–20

For each question, choose the correct answer.

---

16 You will hear a father talking to his son.
What does he want his son to do?

   A tidy the living room

   B tidy the kitchen

   C tidy the bathroom

17 You will hear a girl talking.
Why does she feel bad?

   A Because she had a late night.

   B Because she watched a horror film.

   C Because of something she ate.

18 You will hear Skye talking to her dad.
Where are they?

   A at home

   B in a shop

   C in a café

19 You will hear a man talking about his day.
What is his job?

   A He is a teacher.

   B He is a doctor.

   C He is a businessman.

20 You will hear two students talking about a school club.
Which club have they been to?

   A photography club

   B cooking club

   C cycling club

Part 5

Questions 21–25

For each question, choose the correct answer.

You will hear two parents talking about the new school year.
What do their children need?

Example:

0   Julia | B |

Children

21   Paul   ☐

22   Mickey   ☐

23   Tatum   ☐

24   Zoe   ☐

25   Linda   ☐

Things for school

A a watch

B shoes

C a backpack

D paint brushes

E school uniform

F glasses

G sports clothes

H a coat

Test 6 SPEAKING

You are Candidate B. Answer the questions.

41–42

Do you like these different family days out?

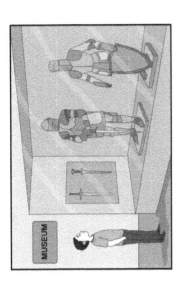

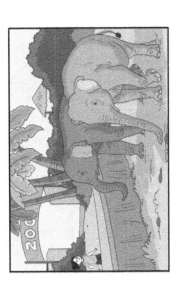

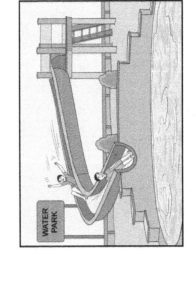

Audio scripts on pages 166–193 and Model answers on pages 205–221.

Test 7

TEST 7 READING AND WRITING

Part 1

Questions 1-6

For each question, choose the correct answer.

1

Books Wanted!

Textbooks or story books
New or used

Top prices paid
Call 01234 765222

A If you want to buy some books, call this phone number.

B If you want to sell some books, call this phone number.

C Call this phone number if you are looking for new or used books.

2

Kevin,

Mark needs a lift home from school. Can you do it? That would help me because I'm in a meeting until 5.

Linda

A Linda wants Mark to pick up Kevin.

B Linda wants Kevin to pick her up.

C Linda wants Kevin to pick up Mark.

3

Hi Ian,

I know you've got lots of homework, but it would be great to share ideas about our project by Friday afternoon.

Mark

A Mark wants Ian to say what he thinks about the project before the weekend.

B Ian has a lot of homework, so Mark wants to help him with the project.

C Mark thinks the ideas that Ian shared with him about the project are great.

4

Tourist Information Centre

All guided tours of the city are fully booked until Monday.

A Guided tours of the city are not available on Monday.

B Tourists can have a guided tour of the city before Monday.

C Guided tours of the city are available on Monday.

5

Hi Jen,

Please tell Mrs Kent I might be late for the game after school. I have to take my sister home first.

Paula

A Paula has to help a member of her family after school.

B Paula will leave the game early to take her sister home.

C Paula wants Jen to take her sister home for her.

6

To: Head Teacher

From: Jane Smith

Dear Sir,

I am writing about the new school uniform. I think it is expensive and it looks untidy.

A Mrs Smith likes the new school uniform.

B Mrs Smith doesn't like the new school uniform.

C Mrs Smith likes the new school uniform, but it costs too much.

Part 2

Questions 7–13

For each question, choose the correct answer.

		Lisa	Mandy	Jin
7	Who doesn't play a musical instrument?	A	B	C
8	Who is different from other members of her family?	A	B	C
9	Who likes listening to three types of music?	A	B	C
10	Who would like to go to more concerts?	A	B	C
11	Who doesn't play only in school concerts?	A	B	C
12	Who always knew she would play a musical instrument one day?	A	B	C
13	Who plays two musical instruments?	A	B	C

Three students talk about their love for music

A Lisa

Music has always been important to me. I grew up in a home where everybody loves music. My parents and my older brothers and sisters all play two or more musical instruments. I didn't have to ask myself if I wanted to play an instrument; it was just a question of which one. I chose the violin and I play in the school orchestra. I play only the violin because I want to be really good at it and I haven't got time to practise another instrument.

B Mandy

I love music and I listen to it all the time. I had piano lessons for a while, but I haven't touched a piano for two years. I prefer listening to music than making it – other people can play much better than I can! The only music I'm not keen on is classical music. I like pop, rock and hip hop, but hip hop is my favourite. I love going to concerts, but that's difficult because of where I live.

C Jin

Everybody in my family loves music. I spent years learning to play the classical guitar, but one instrument isn't enough for me, so I'm taking violin lessons too. I play the violin in school concerts and it's fun to dress smartly and be part of a big group of people all making music together in a concert. I also play the electric guitar in a band with my friends. It's great to turn up the volume so the music is loud!

Part 3

Questions 14–18

For each question, choose the correct answer.

William Shakespeare: The Greatest Writer in the English Language

by Amber Clarke, 13

William Shakespeare (1564–1616) is often said to be the greatest writer in the English language. He wrote at least 37 plays and wrote several more with other people. He also wrote five long poems and 154 shorter ones. His work has been translated into many languages and people still study and discuss it today.

Shakespeare was born in Stratford-upon-Avon and grew up there. He married Anne Hathaway when he was 18 years old and she was 26. They had three children. The details of his life are not clear, partly because he lived a long time ago. However, we know that he had a successful career in London as an actor and a writer.

The stories in Shakespeare's history plays are usually not original. He wrote many plays about real kings and queens, but he didn't try to show what actually happened in history. He used some events to tell his own interesting stories.

Shakespeare also wrote comedies. One of his best known comedies is *Twelfth Night*, where funny things happen because people make mistakes about who other people are. *Much Ado About Nothing* is another play in which people make mistakes about other people's identity. This idea is repeated in many of Shakespeare's comedies.

Shakespeare's plays were first shown at The Globe theatre. It was burnt down in 1613, but a new theatre with the same name has been built nearby. The builders used old pictures of The Globe because they wanted the new theatre to look the same.

14 William Shakespeare

    A usually wrote his plays with other people.

    B worked on more than 37 plays.

    C wrote 154 poems with five other people.

15 We know

    A that Shakespeare was eight years younger than his wife.

    B no details about Shakespeare's life before he went to London.

    C that Shakespeare went to London to become an actor.

16 Shakespeare's plays

    A do not show any facts about kings and queens.

    B are about the interesting events that happened in history.

    C do not always show what really happened in history.

17 Shakespeare's comedies

    A are often about people who think that somebody is somebody else.

    B are funny because the ideas in them are often repeated.

    C are his best known plays.

18 The new theatre

    A is called the Shakespeare Theatre.

    B was built on top of the old theatre.

    C is also called The Globe.

Part 4

Questions 19–24

For each question, choose the correct answer.

Bear Grylls

Edward Michael 'Bear' Grylls is a man who loves danger. He has had many adventures in interesting places and he has written books and **(19)** .... television programmes about them.

Grylls was born in London in 1974. He has one older sister who **(20)** .... him the nickname 'Bear' when he was a baby. From an early age he learned to climb mountains, **(21)** .... boats and jump out of planes.

Grylls climbed Mount Everest in 1998. In 2003 he **(22)** .... the Atlantic Ocean in an open boat. In 2005 he and two other people **(23)** .... a dinner party 7,600 metres up in the air – in a hot-air balloon. These are just a few of the things he has done.

Today he **(24)** .... to have adventures and he is also a successful businessman.

19	**A** acted	**B** done	**C** made
20	**A** became	**B** gave	**C** suggested
21	**A** ride	**B** sail	**C** drive
22	**A** crossed	**B** came	**C** covered
23	**A** had	**B** ate	**C** invited
24	**A** completes	**B** carries	**C** continues

Part 5

Questions 25–30

For each question, write the correct answer.
Write **one** word for each gap.

Example:
0	*your*

> **EMAIL**
>
> From: Adam
>
> To: Kyle
>
> Hi Kyle,
>
> Have you done **(0)** .... work for our group's class talk tomorrow? I've done **(25)** .... part, and Teresa has done hers.
>
> Have you got a good laptop and can you bring it to school tomorrow? **(26)** .... would be good to have one for the talk. My laptop is really old and slow and Teresa hasn't got **(27)** .... at all.
>
> I'm feeling scared. What **(28)** .... you? Do you get nervous before a class talk? I hate it when everybody in the room **(29)** .... looking at me! I hope I can sleep when I go **(30)** .... bed tonight!
>
> Adam

Part 6

Question 31

Your friend Bailey is going to the library. You would like her to take a book back for you. Write a note to Bailey.

In your note:

- ask her to take your book back to the library for you
- say why you can't go to the library yourself
- suggest something that you could do for her in return.

Write **25 words** or more.

Write the note on your answer sheet.

Part 7

Question 32

Look at the three pictures.
Write the story shown in the pictures.
Write **35 words** or more.

Write the story on your answer sheet.

TEST 7 LISTENING

Part 1

Questions 1–5

For each question, choose the correct answer.

---

1 What pet will the children get?

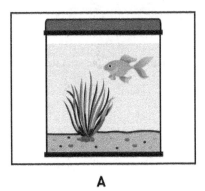

A

B

C

2 Where is Polly's ruler?

A

B

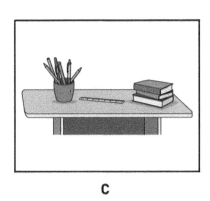

C

3 What will the boy take to the picnic?

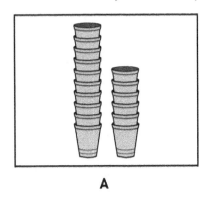

A

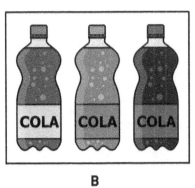

B

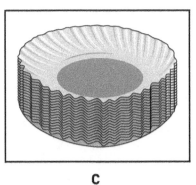

C

4   What has Larry got?

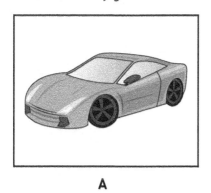   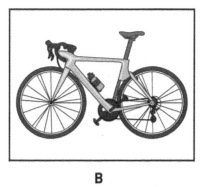   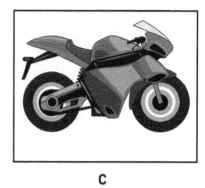

A   B   C

5   What shoes does the girl want?

      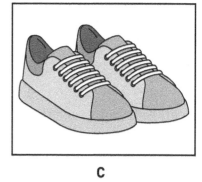

A   B   C

Part 2

Questions 6–10

For each question, write the correct answer in the gap. Write **one word** or **a number** or **a date** or **a time**.

You will hear a student giving a talk about the longest bridge in the world.

The world's longest bridge

Bridge is in:	China
Length of bridge:	**(6)** .... km
Bridge is used by:	**(7)** ....
Year the bridge opened:	**(8)** ....
Bridge goes over fields, rivers and:	a **(9)** ....
China also has a long bridge made of:	**(10)** ....

Part 3

45

Questions 11–15

For each question, choose the correct answer.

You will hear Trevor talking to Melanie about a visit to a museum

11 The museum

    A opens only a few days a week.

    B is next to the old cinema.

    C is opposite the library.

12 Trevor

    A thinks that most museums are interesting.

    B thinks that most museums are boring.

    C would like to see more dinosaurs.

13 At the museum there is a room

    A without a ceiling where you can look at the sky.

    B which shows you the sky at night.

    C which shows you different sorts of lights.

14 The museum

    A was not busy when Trevor went.

    B was too quiet.

    C is not for young children.

15 Trevor thinks Melanie should

    A not go to the museum at the weekend.

    B go to the museum next weekend.

    C go to the museum this weekend.

Part 4

46

Questions 16–20

For each question, choose the correct answer.

---

16 You will hear two parents talking.
Where are they?

    A in the mountains

    B at home

    C at the beach

17 You will hear a boy talking about an evening at the cinema.
What was the problem?

    A Other people were talking.

    B He couldn't see well.

    C The film was boring.

18 You will hear a brother and sister talking in a café.
What is the girl going to have?

    A some juice

    B some pasta

    C a piece of cake

19 You will hear a head teacher talking to a student.
What is the problem?

    A The student is always late for lessons.

    B The student doesn't do his homework.

    C The student talks in class.

20 You will hear a teacher talking in class.
What subject does she teach?

    A art

    B geography

    C science

Part 5

Questions 21–25

For each question, choose the correct answer.

Two parents are looking through a cupboard full of things that belonged to their children a long time ago. Who did the things belong to?

Example:

0 Max | E |

Children

21 Emma ☐

22 Alfie ☐

23 Daniel ☐

24 Lea ☐

25 Jan ☐

Things in the cupboard

A jewellery

B clothes

C toys

D photograph album

E books

F football

G musical instrument

H camping equipment

TEST 7 SPEAKING

You are Candidate B. Answer the questions.

48–49

Do you like these different jobs?

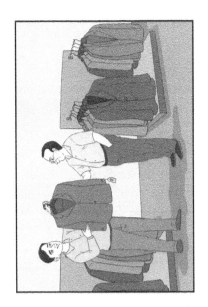

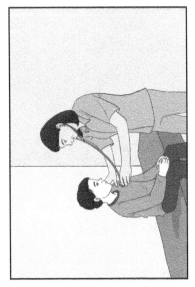

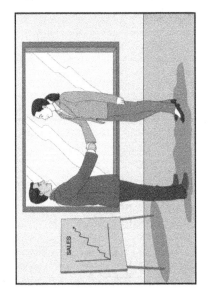

Audio scripts on pages 166–193 and Model answers on pages 205–221.

Test 8

TEST 8 READING AND WRITING

Part 1

Questions 1–6

For each question, choose the correct answer.

1

Hi Jenny,

My plane is leaving in a minute. It was lovely to see you! Next time you should come to us!

Laura

A Laura has visited Jenny.

B Laura is going to visit Jenny.

C Jenny is going to visit Laura.

2

Brown's Store

Ground floor: Children's clothes

First floor: Adults' clothes

Second floor: Home and Kitchen

A If you want women's shoes, go to the ground floor.

B If you want plates and glasses, go to the second floor.

C If you want shirts for boys, go to the first floor.

3

To: Henry
From: Monty

Hi Henry,

Can you look at my laptop? I'm having problems and Sheila told me you're good with them.

Monty

A Sheila is good with computers.

B Monty is having problems with Sheila.

C Henry can repair computers.

4

Hannah, you said you'd let me know if you were coming to my house after school. Have you decided yet?

Jessica

A Jessica wants to know if Hannah is going to visit her.

B Jessica is going to Hannah's house after school.

C Hannah has decided to visit Jessica.

5

School's Out!
magazine

Available now!

Need ideas for the school holidays? See *School's Out!*

A *School's Out!* has suggestions for activities during the school holidays.

B *School's Out!* needs ideas for activities during the school holidays.

C *School's Out!* has ideas for activities at school.

6

To: Parents

From: School Office

Dear parents,

Please make sure your children look smart for the school photographs on Friday.

Thank you.

A The children looked smart for the school photographs on Friday.

B School photographs will be taken on Friday.

C The school office is asking parents to take a photograph of their children on Friday.

Part 2

Questions 7–13

For each question, choose the correct answer.

		Malcolm	Jason	Hamza
7	Who was the youngest when they first met their teacher?	A	B	C
8	Who had to do something in front of other people?	A	B	C
9	Whose teacher helped him when he was hurt?	A	B	C
10	Who says what other students felt about their teacher?	A	B	C
11	Whose teacher taught him something important?	A	B	C
12	Who had their teacher for the longest time?	A	B	C
13	Who wants to try something again after a bad experience?	A	B	C

Three students talk about a teacher they will never forget

A Malcolm

I will never forget Mrs Miller. She was the first teacher I had at primary school. On my very first day at school, I fell in the playground and she picked me up. I was crying and she took me to the school nurse. My knee was bleeding and she sat with me while the nurse put a bandage on it. I was in her class for a year and she was kind to everybody. She never got angry or shouted.

B Jason

I will never forget one of my teachers, Mr Frank, but not for good reasons. He was very strict and all his pupils were scared of him. He taught me music for the last three years of primary school. I stopped studying music because of him. I think music should be fun, but I was scared of playing the wrong note because Mr Frank always shouted at me. But now I am ready to start learning an instrument again with a kinder teacher.

C Hamza

I will always remember Mr Parkhurst. He was my class teacher in my last year of primary school. I was in the school play and I had to stand on my own in the middle of the stage and sing. I got really nervous and I asked if somebody else could do the song. But Mr Parkhurst talked to me and showed me that I could do it. After that, I knew that if I tried, I could do anything. That is why I will always remember him.

Part 3

Questions 14–18

For each question, choose the correct answer.

Life in the snow

by Thomas Everill

Inuit are people who live mostly in the north of Canada, parts of Alaska and Greenland, and they have learned to live in a cold and difficult climate. In this part of the world, the temperature can fall to −45°C in the winter and there is snow for most of the year.

In the past, Inuit lived simple but hard lives. They made their own clothes, built their own houses, and hunted animals and fished for food. They used teams of dogs to pull their sleds over the snow and ice when they needed to travel.

Inuit made round winter homes called igloos using blocks of snow. An experienced person could build an igloo in an hour. The temperature inside an igloo was quite warm even without a fire, simply from a person's body heat. In the summer, the Inuit lived in tent-like homes.

Because of the cold climate, the Inuit diet was almost completely fish and meat. Most people have to eat fruit and vegetables to stay healthy, but over thousands of years, the Inuits' bodies changed so they could be healthy without fruit and vegetables.

Today Inuit life has changed. People use technology and live and work in the modern world. But as the world gets warmer, it is becoming more difficult to hunt animals. There is less ice, so it is harder to travel and the weather changes more quickly. These problems mean it is now safer and easier to buy food from a shop.

14 Inuit live in places where

    A the temperature is –45°C for most of the year.

    B there is snow for many months of the year.

    C other people have not learned to live.

15 In the past, Inuit

    A kept a lot of dogs as pets.

    B had races with teams of dogs in the winter.

    C made and found everything they needed themselves.

16 Inuit

    A made winter homes that were warm.

    B built homes inside blocks of snow.

    C lived in igloos all year.

17 Inuit

    A can be healthy even if they eat only fish and meat.

    B are healthy because they eat a lot of fish and meat.

    C need more than fish and meat to be healthy.

18 These days

    A Inuit want to use more technology and have more modern lives.

    B hunting is easier than going to a shop.

    C less ice means it is more difficult for Inuit to hunt.

Part 4

Questions 19–24

For each question, choose the correct answer.

Summerhill School

Summerhill School in England was founded in 1921, so it is now
(19) .... 100 years old. Most students live at the school. They
have to get up in the morning and **(20)** .... their clothes by
8.30 a.m. but they are more free than students at other schools.
Teachers don't **(21)** .... students what to do. The school allows
students to choose what they want to study, so they make their own
(22) .... They can also decide not to go to lessons if they prefer.
The school is in the countryside and students can play in the woods
and **(23)** .... around it.

Some people think this is a strange way to educate children, but
the school believes it **(24)** .... its students very well for life.

19	**A** off	**B** more	**C** over
20	**A** turn on	**B** put on	**C** get on
21	**A** talk	**B** say	**C** tell
22	**A** timetable	**B** menu	**C** diary
23	**A** factories	**B** fields	**C** banks
24	**A** prepares	**B** grows	**C** explains

Part 5

Questions 25–30

For each question, write the correct answer.
Write **one** word for each gap.

Example: | **0** | *never* |

> **EMAIL**
>
> From: Emily
>
> To: Diana
>
> Hi Diana,
>
> We've **(0)** .... met, but Jane Williams gave me
> your email address. She said that you play the drums
> and that you're looking **(25)** .... a band to play
> with. I play the electric guitar **(26)** .... my friend
> Dave is a singer. We want to find people to play music
> with us. What kind of music **(27)** .... you like?
> How good are you? We're OK, **(28)** .... we aren't
> very good. We want to have fun when we play and we
> don't want to **(29)** .... too serious! **(30)** ....
> you're interested, call me. Here's my mobile number:
> 0888 456789.
>
> Emily Morris

Part 6

Question 31

You friend Ben has asked you to go to the cinema on Saturday. You already have plans and you cannot go.
Write an email to Ben.

In your email:

- explain that you cannot go to the cinema on Saturday

- say what your plans are

- suggest another time to go to the cinema.

Write **25 words** or more.

Write the email on your answer sheet.

Part 7

Question 32

Look at the three pictures.
Write the story shown in the pictures.
Write **35 words** or more.

TEST 8 LISTENING

Part 1

50

Questions 1–5

For each question, choose the correct answer.

---

1 What can't Mona find?

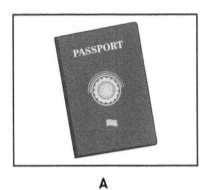

A   B   C

2 What days does Katie have to take the dog for a walk?

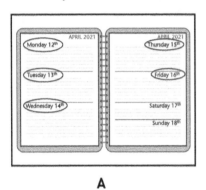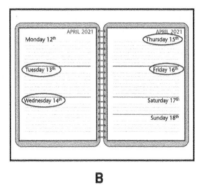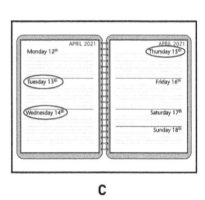

A   B   C

3 How will Jamie and Linda get to the park?

A   B   C

4   What is David painting?

   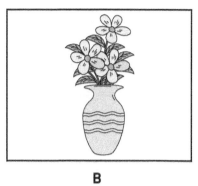   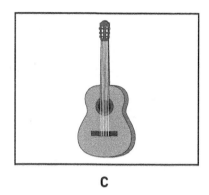

A   B   C

5   What will Tommy wear?

   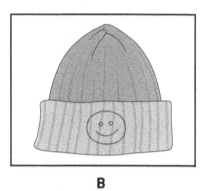   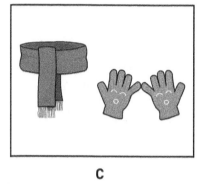

A   B   C

Part 2

51

Questions 6–10

For each question, write the correct answer in the gap. Write **one word** or **a number** or **a date** or **a time**.

You will hear a school nurse talking to students at the beginning of the school year.

Information from the school nurse

If you are ill in the morning: stay at home!

Room number: **(6)** ....

The nurse is available: 9 a.m. **(7)** .... p.m.

If a student is badly hurt, call: **(8)** ....

The nurse can't give students: **(9)** ....

You can also see the nurse if you are: **(10)** ....

Part 3

Questions 11–15

For each question, choose the correct answer.

You will hear Adriana talking to Felix about a bicycle ride she went on.

11 Adriana

    A went on a bicycle ride with a friend.

    B went on a bicycle ride with a group of friends.

    C would like to go cycling on her own.

12 Adriana says that

    A they cycled quickly.

    B they didn't cycle very fast.

    C they got home at about three o'clock.

13 Adriana and Mina

    A began their bicycle ride at Adriana's house.

    B started their bicycle ride at the forest.

    C walked and cycled to the sea.

14 They

    A took the same road on the way back.

    B cycled back using the main road.

    C came back a different way.

15 Adriana says that

    A they didn't take a picnic because they hadn't planned their bicycle ride.

    B they didn't have time for fish and chips by the sea.

    C they took some food with them at the last minute.

Part 4

Questions 16–20

For each question, choose the correct answer.

---

16 You will hear a girl talking.
What does she need?

A a new book

B new glasses

C new clothes

17 You will hear a brother and sister talking about a birthday present for their mother.
What are they looking at?

A chocolates

B flowers

C soap

18 You will hear a mother talking to her child.
Where are they?

A in a clothes shop

B at the swimming pool

C at home

19 You will hear two students talking about somebody.
Who are they talking about?

A a teacher

B a student

C a parent

20 You will hear two students talking.
Where are they?

A on a bus

B at the cinema

C at school

Part 5

54

Questions 21–25

For each question, choose the correct answer.

You will hear two friends talking about a school holiday.
Where do their friends want to go?

Example:

0 Lisa $\boxed{\text{G}}$

People

21 Glen   ☐

22 Kim   ☐

23 Haruko   ☐

24 Terry   ☐

25 Sam   ☐

Places

A the forest

B the museum

C the swimming pool

D the cinema

E the sports centre

F the lake

G the department store

H the theatre

Test 8 SPEAKING

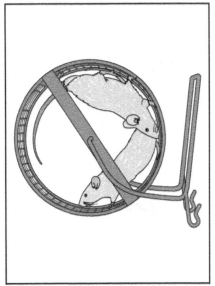

Do you like these different pets?

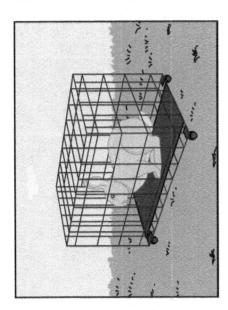

Audio scripts on pages 166–193 and Model answers on pages 205–221.

Mini-dictionary

 Here are some of the more difficult words from the practice tests. Definitions and examples are from *Collins COBUILD* Dictionaries.

TEST 1

bathe /beɪð/ **(bathes, bathing, bathed)** VERB If you **bathe**, you swim. • *Every morning, we bathed in the river.*

believe /bɪˈliːv/ **(believes, believing, believed)** PHRASE You can say **believe it or not** if what you have just said is surprising. • *Believe it or not, he turns 50 next month!*

charity /ˈtʃærɪti/ **(charities)** NOUN A **charity** is an organisation that collects money for people who need help. • *She gives a lot of money to charity.*

colourful /ˈkʌləfʊl/ ADJECTIVE Something that is **colourful** has bright colours or a lot of different colours. • *The people wore colourful clothes.*

court /kɔːt/ **(courts)** NOUN A **court** is an area for playing a game such as tennis or basketball. • *The hotel has several tennis courts.*

cultural /ˈkʌltʃərəl/ ADJECTIVE **Cultural** means to do with the arts. • *We've organised lots of cultural events.*

economic /ˌiːkəˈnɒmɪk, ˌek-/ ADJECTIVE **Economic** means to do with the organisation of the money and industry in a country. • *The economic situation is very bad.*

education /ˌedʒʊˈkeɪʃən/ NOUN **Education** is teaching and learning. • *Education is important to me.*

everyday /ˈevrɪˌdeɪ/ ADJECTIVE Something that is **everyday** is a normal part of your life. • *Computers are a big part of everyday life.*

excellent /ˈeksələnt/ ADJECTIVE Something that is **excellent** is really good. • *The food is excellent.*

feed /fiːd/ **(feeds, feeding, fed)** VERB If you **feed** a person or animal, you give food to them. • *It's usually best to feed a small dog twice a day.*

human being /ˌhjuːmən ˈbiːɪŋ/ **(human beings)** NOUN A **human being** is a man, a woman or a child. • *This shows what human beings are able to do.*

location /ləʊˈkeɪʃən/ **(locations)** NOUN The **location** of something is where it is. • *The hotel has a beautiful location.*

nowadays /ˈnaʊəˌdeɪz/ ADVERB **Nowadays** means now, and not in the past. • *Nowadays many children spend their time playing computer games.*

range /reɪndʒ/ **(ranges, ranging, ranged)** VERB If things **range**, they go from one end of a group of numbers to the other. • *The children range in age from five to fourteen.*

region /ˈriːdʒən/ **(regions)** NOUN A **region** is an area of a country. • *Do you have a map of the region?*

regularly /ˈregjʊləli/ ADVERB If something happens **regularly**, it happens often. • *He writes regularly for the magazine.*

spring /sprɪŋ/ **(springs)** NOUN A **spring** is a place where water comes up through the ground. • *The town is famous for its hot springs.*

tank /tæŋk/ **(tanks)** NOUN A **tank** is a glass bowl which holds water. • *She had a tank full of goldfish.*

tiny /ˈtaɪni/ **(tinier, tiniest)** ADJECTIVE Something that is **tiny** is really small. • *The living room is tiny.*

TEST 2

collar /ˈkɒlə/ **(collars)** NOUN The **collar** of a shirt is the part that goes around your neck. • *His tie was loose and his collar hung open.*

drop /drɒp/ **(drops, dropping, dropped)** VERB If something **is dropped** from an event, it is no longer part of that event. • *Baseball was dropped from the competition.*

forwards /ˈfɔːwədz/ ADVERB **Forwards** means in a direction that is in front of you. • *She fell forwards onto her face.*

however /haʊˈevə/ ADVERB You use **however** when you are saying something that is not expected because of what you have just said. • *The flat is rather small. It is, however, much nicer than our old flat.*

knee /niː/ **(knees)** NOUN Your **knee** is the part in the middle of your leg where it bends. • *Lie down and bring your knees up towards your chest.*

krill /krɪl/ NOUN **Krill** are small animals that live in the sea and are food for some whales. • *Whales take in krill through their huge mouths.*

ocean /ˈəʊʃən/ **(oceans)** NOUN An **ocean** is one of the five very large areas of salt water on the Earth. • *I would like to swim in the ocean.*

place /pleɪs/ PHRASE If something **takes place**, it happens. • *The meeting took place in Paris.*

proper /ˈprɒpə/ ADJECTIVE **Proper** means correct or sensible. • *I think I'll need some proper shoes.*

rule /ruːl/ **(rules)** NOUN A **rule** is something that tells you what you must do or must not do. • *I need a book that explains the rules of basketball.*

score /skɔː/ **(scores, scoring, scored)** VERB If you **score** a goal or a point in a sport or game, you get a goal or point. • *Kerr scored her second goal of the game.*

smart /smɑːt/ ADJECTIVE Someone or something that is **smart** is clean and tidy. • *He looked very smart in his new uniform.*

strict /strɪkt/ ADJECTIVE If someone is **strict**, they think you have to do what they say. • *My parents were very strict.*

swallow /ˈswɒləʊ/ **(swallows, swallowing, swallowed)** VERB When you **swallow**, you make something go from your mouth down into your stomach. • *Polly took a bite of the apple and swallowed it.*

tongue /tʌŋ/ **(tongues)** NOUN Your **tongue** is the soft part inside your mouth that moves when you speak or eat. • *I could taste the salt on my tongue.*

weigh /weɪ/ **(weighs, weighing, weighed)** VERB If someone or something **weighs** a certain amount, they are that heavy. • *It weighs 10 kilos.*

TEST 3

amount /əˈmaʊnt/ **(amounts)** NOUN An **amount** of something is how much of that thing there is or how much of it you have or need. • *He needs that amount of money to live.*

crash /kræʃ/ **(crashes, crashing, crashed)** VERB If a car or aeroplane **crashes**, it hits something. • *Her car crashed into the back of a lorry.*

divide /dɪˈvaɪd/ **(divides, dividing, divided)** VERB If you **divide** something, you break it into smaller parts. • *Divide the pastry in half.*

fuel /ˈfjuːəl/ NOUN **Fuel** is something that burns to give heat or power. • *They bought some fuel on the motorway.*

luckily /ˈlʌkɪli/ ADVERB You use **luckily** when you want to say that it is good that something happened. • *Luckily, nobody was hurt in the accident.*

national park /ˌnæʃnəl ˈpɑːk/ **(national parks)** NOUN A **national park** is a large piece of land which has beautiful scenery and wildlife. It is looked after by the government but people can visit it. • *There are 16 national parks in Alaska.*

nervous /ˈnɜːvəs/ ADJECTIVE If you are **nervous**, you are frightened or worried. • *I was very nervous during the school play.*

ordinary /ˈɔːdɪnri/ ADJECTIVE Something that is **ordinary** is normal and not special or different. • *These are just ordinary people living ordinary lives.*

reach /riːtʃ/ **(reaches, reaching, reached)** VERB If something **reaches** a certain level or amount, it gets to that level or amount. • *Air pollution in the city reached very high levels.*

revise /rɪˈvaɪz/ **(revises, revising, revised)** VERB If you **revise**, you study for an exam. • *I have to revise for my maths exam.*

ruins /ˈruːɪnz/ PLURAL NOUN **Ruins** are the parts of a building that are still there when the rest has fallen down. • *Police found old photographs in the ruins of the house.*

speed of sound /spiːd əv ˈsaʊnd/ NOUN The **speed of sound** is used to talk about how fast sound waves can travel. • *It could fly at twice the speed of sound.*

stay up /steɪ ˈʌp/ **(stays up, staying up, stayed up)** PHRASAL VERB If you **stay up**, you do not go to bed at your usual time. • *I used to stay up late with my mum and watch films.*

topic /ˈtɒpɪk/ **(topics)** NOUN A **topic** is a certain subject that you learn or write about. • *What is the topic of your essay?*

turn /tɜːn/ **(turns)** PHRASE When two or more people **take turns**, they do something one after the other several times. • *We all took turns being at the front.*

TEST 4

attend /əˈtend/ **(attends, attending, attended)** VERB If you **attend** a school or church, you go there regularly. • *They attended college together.*

average /ˈævərɪdʒ/ ADJECTIVE An **average** person or thing is normal. • *The average person doesn't do enough exercise.*

breathe /briːð/ **(breathes, breathing, breathed)** VERB When you **breathe**, you take air in through your mouth or nose and let it out again. • *He was breathing fast.*

ceremony /ˈserɪməni/ **(ceremonies)** NOUN A **ceremony** is a serious and important event. • *The opening ceremony is on Friday night.*

damage /ˈdæmɪdʒ/ **(damages, damaging, damaged)** VERB If you **damage** something, you break it. • *He felt sure he'd damaged the car.*

golf course /ˈɡɒlf kɔːs/ **(golf courses)** NOUN A **golf course** is a large area of grass where people play golf. • *They built a golf course behind the hotel.*

landline /ˈlændlaɪn/ **(landlines)** NOUN A **landline** is a phone that uses cables (= thick wires for carrying electricity), rather than a mobile phone. • *Some people no longer use a landline.*

pleasant /ˈplezənt/ ADJECTIVE A **pleasant** person, thing or event is nice. • *We enjoyed the pleasant weather yesterday.*

pond /pɒnd/ **(ponds)** NOUN A **pond** is a small area of water. • *We sat on a bench beside the duck pond.*

score /skɔː/ **(scores, scoring, scored)** VERB *See Test 2.*

TEST 5

body /ˈbɒdi/ **(bodies)** NOUN You use **body** to talk about a dead person or animal. • *Two days later, her body was found in a wood.*

bring up /brɪŋ ˈʌp/ **(brings up, bringing up, brought up)** PHRASAL VERB If you **bring** a child **up**, you take care of them until they are an adult. • *She brought up four children.*

culture /ˈkʌltʃə/ **(cultures)** NOUN **Culture** is the way of life of a certain group of people, and what they believe in. • *I live with people from different cultures.*

face to face /ˌfeɪs tə ˈfeɪs/ ADVERB When two people meet **face to face**, they meet in person and not online. • *meet face to face*

however /haʊˈevə/ ADVERB *See Test 2.*

imagine /ɪˈmædʒɪn/ **(imagines, imagining, imagined)** VERB If you **imagine** something, you get a picture of it in your head. • *He could not imagine a more beautiful view.*

materials /məˈtɪəriəlz/ PLURAL NOUN **Materials** are the things that you need to do a certain activity. • *There are no books or teaching materials.*

reach /riːtʃ/ **(reaches, reaching, reached)** VERB When you **reach** somewhere, you arrive there. • *He did not stop until he reached the door.*

relative /ˈrelətɪv/ **(relatives)** NOUN Your **relatives** are members of your family. • *All our friends and relatives came to the party.*

remote /rɪˈməʊt/ ADJECTIVE A **remote** place is far away from cities and places where most people live. • *They came from remote villages.*

respect /rɪˈspekt/ **(respects, respecting, respected)** VERB If you **respect** someone, you think very well of them. • *I want people to respect me for my work.*

set up /set ˈʌp/ **(sets up, setting up, set up)** PHRASAL VERB If you **set up** a business, you start it. • *He plans to set up his own business.*

study /ˈstʌdi/ **(studies)** NOUN A **study** is a room in a house that is used for reading, writing and studying. • *We sat together in his study.*

support /səˈpɔːt/ NOUN If someone has **support**, other people help them. • *She gave me a lot of support when I left home.*

turn /tɜːn/ **(turns)** NOUN Your **turn** is the time when you can do something. • *Tonight it's my turn to cook.*

unlike /ʌnˈlaɪk/ PREPOSITION You use **unlike** to say that one person or thing is different from another. • *You're so unlike him!*

TEST 6

check on /ˈtʃek ɒn/ **(checks on, checking on, checked on)** PHRASAL VERB If you **check on** someone, you make sure that they are alright. • *Stephen checked on her several times during the night.*

cruise ship /ˈkruːz ʃɪp/ **(cruise ships)** NOUN A **cruise ship** is a large ship that takes people from place to place as a holiday. • *He got a job as a singer on a cruise ship.*

design /dɪˈzaɪn/ (designs, designing, designed) VERB If someone **designs** something, they make a plan or drawing to show how it should be made. • *The room was designed to hold lots of people.*

floating /ˈfləʊtɪŋ/ ADJECTIVE Something that is **floating** is on top of the water. • *The ship will be used as a floating hotel.*

get on with /get ˈɒn wɪð, wɪθ/ (gets on with, getting on with, got on with) PHRASAL VERB If you **get on with** someone, you are friends with them. • *We've always got on with them very well.*

guided tour /ˌgaɪdɪd ˈtʊə/ (guided tours) NOUN If someone gives you a **guided tour** of a place, they show you the place and tell you about it. • *There is a guided tour every Saturday.*

hardly ever /ˌhɑːdli ˈevə/ PHRASE You use **hardly ever** to mean almost never. • *We hardly ever eat fish.*

luxury /ˈlʌkʃəri/ ADJECTIVE A **luxury** item is expensive and enjoyable, although not something that you need. • *Her fridge is full of luxury food.*

professional /prəˈfeʃənəl/ ADJECTIVE A **professional** sportsperson does sport as a job and not just for fun. • *I would love to be a professional rugby player.*

recently /ˈriːsəntli/ ADVERB If something was done **recently**, it was done only a short time ago. • *We recently moved house.*

regularly /ˈregjʊləli/ ADVERB See Test 1.

TEST 7

fully /ˈfʊli/ ADVERB You use **fully** to mean completely. • *We are fully aware of the problem.*

guided tour /ˌgaɪdɪd ˈtʊə/ (guided tours) NOUN See Test 6.

hot-air balloon /ˌhɒtˈeə bəluːn/ (hot-air balloons) NOUN A **hot-air balloon** is a large balloon filled with hot air with a basket under it in which people can travel. • *Visitors can book a trip in a hot-air balloon.*

however /haʊˈevə/ ADVERB See Test 2.

identity /aɪˈdentɪti/ (identities) NOUN Your **identity** is who you are. • *He uses the name Abu to hide his identity.*

keen /kiːn/ ADJECTIVE If you are **keen on** someone or something, you like them a lot. • *I'm not keen on maths.*

nickname /ˈnɪkneɪm/ (nicknames) NOUN A **nickname** is a fun name for someone or something. • *Red got his nickname for his red hair.*

orchestra /ˈɔːkɪstrə/ (orchestras) NOUN An **orchestra** is a large group of people who play different musical instruments together. • *The orchestra began to play.*

original /əˈrɪdʒɪnəl/ ADJECTIVE Something that is **original** is new and not a copy. • *It is an original piece of writing.*

partly /ˈpɑːtli/ ADVERB You use **partly** to mean not completely. • *It's partly my fault.*

poem /ˈpəʊɪm/ (poems) NOUN A **poem** is a piece of writing in which the words are written in short lines. • *He read to her from a book of love poems.*

smartly /ˈsmɑːtli/ ADVERB Someone who dresses **smartly** is clean and tidy. • *He dressed very smartly, which I liked.*

translate /trænzˈleɪt/ (translates, translating, translated) VERB If someone **translates** something, they say or write it in another language. • *Some of his books have been translated into English.*

volume /ˈvɒljuːm/ NOUN **Volume** is how loud or quiet a sound is. • *He turned down the volume.*

TEST 8

bandage /ˈbændɪdʒ/ (bandages) NOUN A **bandage** is a piece of cloth that you put round a part of your body that is hurt. • *We put a bandage on John's knee.*

bleed /bliːd/ (bleeds, bleeding, bled) VERB If a part of your body **is bleeding**, blood is coming out of it. • *Ian's lip was bleeding.*

block /blɒk/ (blocks) NOUN A **block** of something is a large hard piece of something. • *Elizabeth carves animals from blocks of wood.*

body heat /ˈbɒdi hiːt/ NOUN Your **body heat** is how hot your body is. • *Most body heat is lost through the head.*

diet /ˈdaɪət/ (diets) NOUN Your **diet** is the kind of food that you normally eat. • *It's never too late to improve your diet.*

educate /ˈedʒʊkeɪt/ (educates, educating, educated) VERB To **educate** someone means to teach them. • *He was educated at Oxford.*

found /faʊnd/ **(founds, founding, founded)** VERB
When a place or organisation **is founded**,
someone starts it. • *The charity was founded in
1892.*

hunt /hʌnt/ **(hunts, hunting, hunted)** VERB If people
hunt, they chase and kill wild animals for food.
• *I learned to hunt and fish when I was a child.*

igloo /ˈɪgluː/ **(igloos)** NOUN **Igloos** are small round
houses made from large pieces of hard snow.
• *She knew how to build an igloo.*

mostly /ˈməʊstli/ ADVERB You use **mostly** to mean
almost always. • *My friends are mostly girls.*

nervous /ˈnɜːvəs/ ADJECTIVE If you are **nervous**, you
are frightened or worried. • *I was very nervous
during the school play.*

note /nəʊt/ **(notes)** NOUN In music, a **note** is a
certain sound. • *She can't sing high notes.*

playground /ˈpleɪgraʊnd/ **(playgrounds)** NOUN A
playground is a piece of land where children can
play, especially in a school. • *He hurt himself in
the playground.*

primary school /ˈpraɪməri skuːl/ **(primary schools)**
NOUN A **primary school** is a school for children
between the ages of 4 or 5 and 11. • *She's in her
third year of primary school.*

sled /sled/ **(sleds)** NOUN A **sled** is an object that
you can sit on while it slides over snow. • *He
would need seven dogs to pull the sled.*

strict /strɪkt/ ADJECTIVE *See Test 2.*

Audio scripts

These are the audio scripts for the Listening and Speaking parts of the tests. Listen to the audio online at:
www.collins.co.uk/eltresources

TEST 1   LISTENING

Part 1

Track 01

Key English Test for Schools, Listening.
There are five parts to the test. You will hear each piece twice.
We will now stop for a moment.
Please ask any questions now, because you must not speak during the test.
Now look at the instructions for Part 1.
For each question, choose the correct answer.
Look at Question 1.

1 *What has the boy lost?*

Boy:	I can't find my sports shoes!
Mother:	They're by the front door. With your socks.
Boy:	My socks! I've been looking for them too. Is my T-shirt with them?
Mother:	I've only seen your shoes and socks.
Boy:	Then what can I do about my T-shirt?

Now listen again.

2 *What day is football practice?*

Boy:	Do you want to meet up after school on Tuesday?
Girl:	I'd like to, but I've got a lot of homework to do that evening. The next day would be better.
Boy:	I've got football practice that day. What about Thursday?
Girl:	OK, then. Let's meet up on Thursday after school.
Boy:	All right.

Now listen again.

3 *What sport will Jane do at the sports centre?*

Mark:	Hi Jane. Have you decided what to do at the sports centre? You were thinking about tennis, weren't you?
Jane:	Hi Mark. Yes, but it's so popular it will be difficult to get a court to play on. I think I'll do volleyball.
Mark:	Why don't you do swimming? There's a great pool.
Jane:	Because I'm no good at swimming. I'd get bored.

Now listen again.

4 *How much money does the boy need to buy tickets for the school play?*

Boy:	Dad, do you want to come to the school play?
Father:	Of course I want to come!
Boy:	How many tickets do you want?
Father:	One for me and one for your mum.
Boy:	They're £7.50 each, so that's £15. And if Alice comes, tickets for children are £2.50.
Father:	Alice is too young, so just two tickets. I'll get my wallet.

Now listen again.

5 *What did the girl see on her school trip?*

Mother:	Well, did you have a good trip?
Girl:	It was great! We saw how honey was made.
Mother:	That's fun. So you saw lots of bees.
Girl:	Yes, lots of them. They drink from flowers to make honey. And do you know, birds eat them sometimes!
Mother:	Birds eat bees?! I never knew that!

Now listen again.
That is the end of Part 1.

Part 2

Track 02

Now look at Part 2.
For each question, write the correct answer in the gap.
Write one word or a number or a date, or a time.
Look at Questions 6–10 now. You have ten seconds.
You will hear a teacher giving students information about a visitor who is coming to the school.

Teacher:	Please remember that we have a visitor coming to our school today. He'll be giving a talk to our class about a local business. Please be polite and quiet when he's giving his talk. His name is Mr Macilroy. That's spelled M-A-C-I-L-R-O-Y. He's a very interesting man and you will have the chance to learn some useful information. He's going to talk to us about his café, and this will help you with your school project. He'll be here at eleven fifteen and his talk will last 45 minutes, until twelve. You'll have your lunch break at ten past twelve. You can ask him questions about how he started his business and how many people work for him. Remember, your project must be about 500 words long. Please, not much longer than this, and certainly not shorter. You have until next Friday, Friday 16th April, to hand it in. If you hand it in late, you'll get a lower grade!

Now listen again.
That is the end of Part 2.

Part 3

Track 03

Now look at Part 3.
For each question, choose the correct answer.
Look at Questions 11–15 now.
You have 20 seconds.
You will hear John talking to Monica about his trip to London.

Monica:	Hi John.
John:	Hi Monica.
Monica:	How was your trip to London yesterday? It rained here and the traffic was terrible.
John:	Well, there's always a problem with traffic in London, but I didn't need my umbrella at all! But somebody stole my wallet!
Monica:	Oh no! When did that happen?
John:	Immediately we arrived. We'd just got off the train. So my dad and I spent all morning at the police station telling the police about it.
Monica:	How terrible! Did you lose a lot of money?
John:	I didn't have any cash with me, but I lost my library card and my gym card. My bank card was in my jacket pocket, luckily.
Monica:	What did the police say?
John:	They said I'd be lucky to get my wallet back. They said it was a good idea not to keep my bank card in my wallet and not to carry any cash.
Monica:	Did you have a nice afternoon after that?
John:	Not really. My parents were angry with me for not looking after my wallet and we couldn't agree what to do.
Monica:	Poor you!

Now listen again.
That is the end of Part 3.

Part 4

Track 04

Now look at Part 4.
For each question, choose the correct answer.

16 *You will hear a teacher talking to a student. Why is the teacher angry?*

Teacher:	It's not good enough, David. This is the third time this week.
David:	I'm sorry. It won't happen again.
Teacher:	You said that last time. You must get to class on time.
David:	I'll try. Can I sit down now?
Teacher:	Yes, but don't make it worse by chatting. And hand in your homework.

Now listen again.

17 *You will hear two friends talking. Where have they been?*

Boy 1:	That was brilliant!
Boy 2:	I know. It was so exciting! I didn't know how it was going to finish.
Boy 1:	Anything could have happened. It wasn't a good start for us, but the second half was much better.
Boy 2:	Our players were very lucky, I think. Anyway, we won!

Now listen again.

18 *You will hear a girl talking. Why couldn't she sleep last night?*

Girl:	I'm so tired! I didn't get any sleep last night. We were at a party at my neighbour's house and we got home late. But I was so scared about the test today that I couldn't sleep. My dad was angry with me this morning and said he won't let me go to parties again during the week.

Now listen again.

19 *You will hear two friends planning an activity. What do they decide to do?*

Girl 1:	Well, let's leave the park for another day. What about going down to the beach? Or the swimming pool.
Girl 2:	I'd prefer to swim in the sea than the pool.
Girl 1:	So would I. We can take the bus. There's one in half an hour.

Now listen again.

20 *You will hear a student talking. What has he lost?*

Student:	I can't find it! What am I going to do? I use it for my homework notes and lots of other things. I'll have to call Greg and ask him about homework. And I can't remember what I've planned for tomorrow! Well, at least I've got my mobile and I didn't take my laptop to school.

Now listen again.
That is the end of Part 4.

Part 5

Track 05

Now look at Part 5.
For each question, choose the correct answer.
Look at Questions 21–25 now.
You have 15 seconds.
You will hear two teachers talking about parents' evening at school. What will each student talk about?

Teacher 1:	Is everything ready for the parents' evening?
Teacher 2:	I think so. Dennis has prepared his talk about what the physics and chemistry students learned this year.
Teacher 1:	Great. I saw Helen with all the maps she's going to show. And she's got photos of the mountains and lakes we studied this term.
Teacher 2:	Does Shazad need help with his exhibition about the kings and queens of the last five hundred years?
Teacher 1:	You're getting confused! Shazad is talking about the activities students can do after school. Chess, photography, that sort of thing. Brian is doing the kings and queens.

Teacher 2:   Oh. I just saw Amal. She looked scared, poor girl.

Teacher 1:   Oh, she'll be fine. She's only got a short talk: what students have to wear and what they're not allowed to wear.

Teacher 2:   Yes, but she'll probably get lots of questions from parents.

Teacher 1:   I'm sure she will, but we must make sure there's time for Mary's talk.

Teacher 2:   Yes, I think parents will be interested to hear how long children should spend studying outside class. I had to help Mary with her talk. I mean, she's just a student.

Now listen again.
That is the end of Part 5. You now have six minutes to write your answers on the answer sheet.
That is the end of the test.

TEST 1   SPEAKING

Part 1

Track 06

Examiner: Good morning.
Can I have your mark sheets, please? I'm Frank Green. And this is Julia Turner.
What's your name, Candidate A?

Candidate A: My name's Afonso Silva.

Examiner: And what's your name, Candidate B?

[PAUSE FOR YOU TO ANSWER]

Examiner: Candidate B, how old are you?

[PAUSE FOR YOU TO ANSWER]

Examiner: Where do you live, Candidate B?

[PAUSE FOR YOU TO ANSWER]

Examiner: Thank you.
Candidate A, how old are you?

Candidate A: I'm twelve.

Examiner: Where do you live?

Candidate A: I live in Belem.

Examiner: Thank you.
Now, let's talk about the area where you live.
Candidate A, do you like the area where you live?

Candidate A: Yes, I do. We have nice neighbours. The area is quiet and it's safe. I think it's a good place to live.

Examiner: How long have you lived there?

Candidate A: I've lived there all my life, so I know it very well. A lot of friends also live nearby.

Examiner: Candidate B, what do you like about the area where you live?

[PAUSE FOR YOU TO ANSWER]

Examiner: Is there anything you don't like about your area, Candidate B?

[PAUSE FOR YOU TO ANSWER]

Examiner: Now, Candidate A, please tell me about a place you would like to live if you could live anywhere.

Candidate A: My grandparents have a house in the countryside. It's also very near the sea, so you can go to the beach and swim or you can play in the fields. I'd love to live in that area if I could.

Examiner: Now, let's talk about sleeping. Candidate B, what time do you go to sleep at night?

[PAUSE FOR YOU TO ANSWER]

Examiner: Do you sleep well, Candidate B?

[PAUSE FOR YOU TO ANSWER]

Examiner: Candidate A, do you like sleeping?

Candidate A: Yes, I do. When I go to bed, I read for a little while and then feel sleepy and I'm ready to go to sleep.

Examiner: How much sleep do you need?

Candidate A: I think I need about eight or nine hours. If I sleep from ten or eleven o'clock at night to seven or eight o'clock in the morning, then I feel good.

Examiner: Now, Candidate B, please tell me if you think teenagers get enough sleep.

[PAUSE FOR YOU TO ANSWER]

Examiner: Thank you.

Part 2

Track 07

Examiner: Now, in this part of the test you are going to talk together.
Here are some pictures that show different ways of getting to school. Do you like these different ways of getting to school? Say why or why not. I'll say that again. Do you like these different ways of getting to school? Say why or why not.
All right? Now, talk together.

Candidate A: I think walking is a good way to get to school because it keeps you fit. Do you agree?

[PAUSE FOR YOU TO ANSWER]

Candidate A: What do you think about cycling to school?

[PAUSE FOR YOU TO ANSWER]

Candidate A: No, it isn't. You'd get very wet and you don't want to be wet all day at school. And you have to look after your bike, keep it in good condition so it works well.

[PAUSE FOR YOU TO ANSWER]

Candidate A: What do you think about getting a lift from your parents?

[PAUSE FOR YOU TO ANSWER]

Candidate A:	Well, a lot of children go to school by bus and there's often a bus stop outside a school. Finally, what about going to school by taxi?
[PAUSE FOR YOU TO ANSWER]	
Candidate A:	Yes, I agree with you.
Examiner:	Candidate A, do you like going to school by bus?
Candidate A:	No, I don't.
Examiner:	Why not?
Candidate A:	I like to have a quiet time in the morning, but buses are usually very crowded and noisy. Also, if there are a lot of people on the bus, it isn't a comfortable way to travel.
Examiner:	Candidate B, do you like walking to school?
[PAUSE FOR YOU TO ANSWER]	
Examiner:	So Candidate A, which of these ways of getting to school do you like the best?
Candidate A:	I think walking is the best way – unless the weather is bad.
Examiner:	And you, Candidate B, which of these ways of getting to school do you like the best?
[PAUSE FOR YOU TO ANSWER]	
Examiner:	Thank you. Can I have the booklet, please? Now, Candidate B, can you compare walking to school to getting to school by bus?
[PAUSE FOR YOU TO ANSWER]	
Examiner:	And what about you, Candidate A? Can you compare walking to school with getting a lift from your parents?
Candidate A:	Going to school by car is very comfortable, but it might be boring if you have to go home with them immediately after school. I like to see my friends after school, so I prefer to walk home with them.
Examiner:	Candidate A, which of these ways of getting to school do you think is the worst?
Candidate A:	I think cycling is the worst way.
Examiner:	Why?
Candidate A:	I don't like cycling because I get hot. I also think it's dangerous because of the traffic.
Examiner:	Which of these ways of getting to school do you think is the worst, Candidate B?
[PAUSE FOR YOU TO ANSWER]	
Examiner:	Thank you. That is the end of the test.

TEST 2 LISTENING

Part 1

Track 08

Key English Test for Schools, Listening.
There are five parts to the test. You will hear each piece twice.
We will now stop for a moment.
Please ask any questions now, because you must not speak during the test.
Now look at the instructions for Part 1.
For each question, choose the correct answer.
Look at Question 1.

1 *What will the weather be like at the beach?*

Boy:	Should we take our coats with us to the beach? Do you think it will rain?
Girl:	The news says it's going to be warm and sunny. It's only going to rain later in the week.
Boy:	Good. I hate it when it rains.
Girl:	I think it's even worse when it's windy.

Now listen again.

2 *What is Sophie going to do with her friend?*

Jack:	Hi Sophie. What are you doing today?
Sophie:	Hi Jack. I'm meeting Diana. We wanted to go to the theatre, but we couldn't get tickets.
Jack:	Bad luck.
Sophie:	So we're going to have a snack instead.
Jack:	Where are you going?
Sophie:	The new place next to the cinema.
Jack:	Tell me if you like it.

Now listen again.

3 *What is the boy going to read on the train?*

Girl:	Are you going to bring your book to read on the train?
Boy:	No, I've finished it. Can I borrow one from you?
Girl:	Yes, I've got one you'd really like. It's on the table, there, next to Mum's newspaper and that magazine.
Boy:	Where? Oh, I see. Thanks. Hey, this looks interesting.
Girl:	It is.

Now listen again.

4 *What is the girl going to have at the café?*

Boy:	What are you going to have? I'm going to have a hot chocolate.
Girl:	It's too hot for that. I think I'll have an ice cream.
Boy:	They have good sandwiches here.
Girl:	Hmm, maybe. But Mum says we have to go home for lunch, so a sandwich is too much just now.

Now listen again.

Audio scripts

5 *What time will the football game finish?*

Boy:	Mum, can you pick me up after my football game?
Mum:	What time?
Boy:	Well, the match starts at three, and with half time the game lasts two hours.
Mum:	OK, I'll pick you up on the way home from Granny's.
Boy:	That'll be great, Mum. Thanks a lot.

Now listen again.
That is the end of Part 1.

Part 2

Track 09

Now look at Part 2.
For each question, write the correct answer in the gap.
Write one word or a number or a date or a time. Look at Questions 6–10 now.
You have ten seconds.
You will hear a student giving a talk about honey bees in a biology class.

Student: My class talk today is about honey bees. Most of us like honey, so I wanted to talk about the animals that make it. There are eight different types of honey bee in the world, but in the UK there's only one. Many people think that bees just give us honey, but they're important for other reasons too. Plants need the bees so they can make fruit and vegetables like tomatoes and peas. In fact, farmers in the UK save millions of pounds a year because the bees help their plants so much!
Bees live together in big groups. There's one queen bee and thousands of worker bees. In the autumn and winter, when the temperature goes below ten degrees, honey bees stop flying. The worker bees crowd around the queen bee to keep her warm and they eat the honey they made earlier in the year. Worker bees live 14 to 28 days, but a queen bee can live for two or three years!

Now listen again.
That is the end of Part 2.

Part 3

Track 10

Now look at Part 3.
For each question, choose the correct answer.
Look at Questions 11–15 now.
You have 20 seconds.
You will hear Philippa talking to her friend James about moving house.

James:	Hi Philippa. I hear you're moving.
Philippa:	Yes, because of my dad's job. He nearly lost it! The company closed his office, but

luckily, they moved him to another one. He moved into our new house a few weeks ago.

James:	Are you moving schools too?
Philippa:	I don't have to! The new house isn't far away, actually. It's near the station and I'll be able to take the train to the city centre and walk from there.
James:	That's great! Have you seen the new house?
Philippa:	Yes, it's fantastic! I'll have a bedroom all to myself and I won't have to share with my sister anymore.
James:	Nice. You should have a party at the new house!
Philippa:	My parents wouldn't be happy about that. They like it when things are quiet.
James:	Well, they can go out for the evening and you can have a party until they come home.
Philippa:	Good idea. I'll ask them about it, but I don't know if they'll agree.

Now listen again.
That is the end of Part 3.

Part 4

Track 11

Now look at Part 4.
For each question, choose the correct answer.

16 *You will hear a student talking to a teacher. Why didn't she do her homework?*

Girl:	I'm really sorry. I tried to do my homework, but my sister's not well and my mum and I went to visit her in hospital. It took hours to get there and hours to get back, so I didn't have time. I can do it this evening because we aren't going to visit her today.

Now listen again.

17 *You will hear two friends talking. What are they eating?*

Boy:	Mmm, nice.
Girl:	Not bad, but not as good as a pizza or a burger.
Boy:	Well, we haven't got time for anything hot.
Girl:	I know, but the bread is good. I had a pizza the other day, anyway.
Boy:	And I had a burger the other day too!

Now listen again.

18 *You will hear a boy talking about a film he saw. What was the film like?*

Boy:	You really should see the film if you get the chance. I thought it would be boring because it has a lot of history in it, but it wasn't at all like that. My sister liked it too, and she usually only likes comedies. But this is a serious film. In fact, most of it is very scary.

Now listen again.

19 *You will hear two friends getting ready to play a game. What game are they going to play?*

Boy: Are you ready? Have you got the balls?

Girl: I've got two and there's one next to your foot.

Boy: Only three! We'll have to run around a lot and pick them up all the time.

Girl: The way you hit them, yes, we will.

Boy: Ha ha. OK, they're in the basket. Shall we go?

Now listen again.

20 *You will hear a girl talking about her pet. What sort of animal is it?*

Girl: She's called Coco. She's lovely and really friendly. She isn't like other cats. She's more like a dog because she follows you around and wants to go for walks. I wanted a rabbit at first, but I love Coco now!

Now listen again.
That is the end of Part 4.

Part 5

Track 12

Now look at Part 5.
For each question, choose the correct answer.
Look at Questions 21–25 now.
You have 15 seconds.
You will hear two students talking about their group project. Who will do the different parts of the project?

Girl: We're the group leaders, so we have to decide who does each part of the project. Do we know anybody with a good printer?

Boy: Yes, Oliver has one. He's already said he would do that.

Girl: OK. That's great. Now, Mia's very confident in front of people, isn't she? Let's ask her to read.

Boy: And I think Lucas should work on the front page. He made an excellent advertisement for that other project with the photographs we gave him. I think he could make it look really good.

Girl: Then we need somebody to look at the answers we collected, add all the numbers and make it clear what we learned from the project.

Boy: Mehmet would be good at that.

Girl: Good idea. Now, Ava is good with words. We can give her the information and she can do the text.

Boy: Well, I thought Jess could do that. Then Ava would have the final job of looking through it to make sure everything is correct.

Girl: All right. Now let's tell everybody.

Now listen again.
That is the end of Part 5. You now have six minutes to write your answers on the answer sheet.
That is the end of the test.

TEST 2   SPEAKING

Part 1

Track 13

Examiner: Good afternoon.
Can I have your mark sheets, please?
I'm Meg Gibsy. And this is Scott Stevens.
What's your name, Candidate A?

Candidate A: My name's Magdalena Nowak.

Examiner: And what's your name, Candidate B?

[PAUSE FOR YOU TO ANSWER]

Examiner: Candidate B, how old are you?

[PAUSE FOR YOU TO ANSWER]

Examiner: Where are you from, Candidate B?

[PAUSE FOR YOU TO ANSWER]

Examiner: Thank you.
Candidate A, how old are you?

Candidate A: I'm thirteen.

Examiner: Where are you from?

Candidate A: I'm from Warsaw in Poland.

Examiner: Thank you.
Now, let's talk about presents.
Candidate A, do you like to give or receive presents?

Candidate A: I prefer to receive presents. It's exciting to get them.

Examiner: Who gives you presents and when do they give them to you?

Candidate A: My parents give me presents on my birthday and they also give me presents at Christmas.

Examiner: Candidate B, do you like to give or receive presents?

[PAUSE FOR YOU TO ANSWER]

Examiner: When was the last time you got a present, Candidate B?

[PAUSE FOR YOU TO ANSWER]

Examiner: Now, Candidate A, please tell me about a present that you got that you were really happy with.

Candidate A: My parents gave me a mobile phone on my twelfth birthday and I was very happy to get it. It was my first phone. Before then, they said I was too young to have one.

Examiner: Now, let's talk about your future.
Candidate B, do you know what you would like to do after you have finished school?

[PAUSE FOR YOU TO ANSWER]

Examiner: Where would you like to go to university, Candidate B?

[PAUSE FOR YOU TO ANSWER]

Examiner: Candidate A, do you know what you would like to do after you have finished school?

Candidate A:	Yes, I do. I want to go to university and study to be a doctor.
Examiner:	Why do you want to be a doctor?
Candidate A:	Both my parents are doctors and I think the job they do is very important. They help people when they're sick and I'd like to do that too.
Examiner:	Now, Candidate B, please tell me if you think young people should plan their future carefully.
[PAUSE FOR YOU TO ANSWER]	
Examiner:	Thank you.

Part 2

Track 14

Examiner:	Now, in this part of the test you are going to talk together. Here are some pictures that show different games. Do you like these different games? Say why or why not. I'll say that again. Do you like these different games? Say why or why not. All right? Now, talk together.
Candidate A:	I think badminton is a fun game and I really enjoy playing it. Do you like it?
[PAUSE FOR YOU TO ANSWER]	
Candidate A:	How do you feel about basketball?
[PAUSE FOR YOU TO ANSWER]	
Candidate A:	Yes, you're right. You can practise throwing the ball at the basket even when you're alone. With the other games, you need people to play with you.
[PAUSE FOR YOU TO ANSWER]	
Candidate A:	What about tennis?
[PAUSE FOR YOU TO ANSWER]	
Candidate A:	I think it's a boring game. I played football with my brothers when I was younger. I was the goalkeeper, but I always let the ball go into the net.
[PAUSE FOR YOU TO ANSWER]	
Candidate A:	Yes, that's true. A lot of people can play together.
Examiner:	Candidate A, do you like playing table tennis?
Candidate A:	Yes, I do. It's one of my favourite games.
Examiner:	What do you like about it?
Candidate A:	It's easy to play. Even if you aren't very good, you can have a fun time.
Examiner:	Candidate B, do you like playing table tennis?
[PAUSE FOR YOU TO ANSWER]	
Examiner:	So, Candidate A, which of these games do you like the best?

Candidate A:	I think badminton is the best game. It's easy to play and it doesn't matter if you aren't very good at it.
Examiner:	And you, Candidate B, which of these games do you like the best?
[PAUSE FOR YOU TO ANSWER]	
Examiner:	Thank you. Can I have the booklet, please? Now, Candidate B, can you compare basketball with football?
[PAUSE FOR YOU TO ANSWER]	
Examiner:	And what about you, Candidate A? Can you compare badminton to tennis?
Candidate A:	I think they're very different games. Badminton is slower and easier to play than tennis. You can take your badminton racket anywhere, and you don't have to play with a net. For example, you can even play badminton at the beach. Tennis is more serious and you need to play on a tennis court.
Examiner:	Candidate A, which of these games do you like the least?
Candidate A:	I like football the least.
Examiner:	Why?
Candidate A:	Everybody gets too excited. Everybody shouts at everybody. I don't think it's a nice game.
Examiner:	Which of these games do you like the least, Candidate B?
[PAUSE FOR YOU TO ANSWER]	
Examiner:	Thank you. That is the end of the test.

TEST 3   LISTENING

Part 1

Track 15

Key English Test for Schools, Listening.
There are five parts to the test. You will hear each piece twice.
We will now stop for a moment.
Please ask any questions now, because you must not speak during the test.
Now look at the instructions for Part 1.
For each question, choose the correct answer.
Look at Question 1.

1 *What new clothes does Petra need?*

Mum:	Come on, Petra! We're going shopping for clothes.
Petra:	Oh, Mum! Why? I got a new skirt last week!
Mum:	Yes, and we said it's too short. We're going to change it. You can keep the blouse and the jumper. And next time, don't go shopping without me!

Now listen again.

2 *What is Marcus going to do after school?*

Jen:	Are you ready for the game after school, Marcus?
Marcus:	I can't play. Sorry, Jen.
Jen:	But we changed the day for you! We didn't play yesterday because you said you were going to the dentist.
Marcus:	I know, but I've got an eye test today.
Jen:	Dentist? Eye test? What's next? The doctor?
Marcus:	I haven't been to the doctor for ages.

Now listen again.

3 *When will the girl go on holiday?*

Boy:	Are you still going on holiday in July?
Girl:	Well, my dad can only get time off work in August, not July. But my mum's not happy about August because she says it's too hot then. She'd prefer September.
Boy:	Mmm.
Girl:	But now my aunt's getting married in September, so we can't go then. So, we'll have to go when it's hot!

Now listen again.

4 *Where is the boy's mobile phone?*

Boy:	Oh no! I can't find my phone! Maybe I left it on the bus.
Girl:	You had it in the library. You made a call, remember?
Boy:	That's right – and then we went to the café and I sent Mum a text.
Girl:	There you go. That was the last place you had it.
Boy:	I'm going back on the bus to get it.

Now listen again.

5 *What did the girl have for breakfast?*

Boy:	Would you like something to eat?
Girl:	No, thanks. I've only just had breakfast.
Boy:	I suppose you had a big cooked breakfast?
Girl:	You know me! Mum says I should eat more healthy food, and all week I've only had time for cereal, but not today!

Now listen again.
That is the end of Part 1.

Part 2

Track 16

Now look at Part 2.
For each question, write the correct answer in the gap.
Write one word or a number or a date or a time. Look at Questions 6–10 now.
You have ten seconds.
You will hear a student giving information about school clubs to new students.

Student:	Hello everybody. I'm going to give you some information about the clubs we have at this school. There are lots, and you can

join up to three clubs, but no more than that because the teachers want us to have enough time to do our homework. All the sports clubs are on a Wednesday. There are two times for the sports clubs: from three o'clock to four o'clock and from quarter past four to quarter past five. This is so you can do two different sports, but of course, you can't do two different sports if they're at the same time! The school can't run clubs for small numbers of students, so there must be at least 15 students for a club. Now, some good news. There's a new club this year: art club. If you're interested in it, please send Mrs Schneider an email. Mrs Schneider's name is spelled S-C-H-N-E-I-D-E-R. Most clubs are free, but music club costs £8 a term because we have to bring in somebody from outside the school to run it.

Now listen again.
That is the end of Part 2.

Part 3

Track 17

Now look at Part 3.
For each question, choose the correct answer. Look at Questions 11–15 now.
You have 20 seconds.
You will hear Henry talking to his friend Charlotte about his grandmother.

Charlotte:	Hi Henry. Where are you going?
Henry:	Hi Charlotte. To visit my grandmother. She's been ill and she was in hospital for a while. She's staying with my aunt until she's well enough to go home.
Charlotte:	I hope she's better soon.
Henry:	Thanks. I'll get her some flowers on the way. I was going to get her something nice, like chocolates, but Mum said she can only eat things like soup, fruit and vegetables, and I don't think apples or bananas make a good present!
Charlotte:	Do you see her often?
Henry:	Yes. She lives in a flat on the other side of town. It's on the ground floor, so she doesn't have to use the stairs or the lift.
Charlotte:	Is she very old?
Henry:	She's eighty. She's the only one of her brothers and sisters who's still living. She had four brothers and three sisters!
Charlotte:	That's a lot of brothers and sisters!
Henry:	I don't think it was unusual in those days. People think it's expensive to have children nowadays, but Granny says when she was young, children often worked and brought money home.

Now listen again.
That is the end of Part 3.

Part 4

Track 18

Now look at Part 4.
For each question, choose the correct answer.

16 *You will hear a boy talking about his part-time job. Where does he work?*

Boy: It's OK, but it can be a bit boring sometimes. It's better than the shop I worked in before. I have to make sure people don't touch things because some of them are really old, and I have to ask little kids to be quiet if they're noisy. But it's not like a library, where you have to be really quiet.

Now listen again.

17 *You will hear two girls talking about a new piece of furniture. What is the piece of furniture?*

Girl 1: Ooh! That's nice. I love the colour.
Girl 2: Yes, I like it too, and it's very comfortable.
Girl 1: And big enough for three or four people.
Girl 2: Yes. Good for film nights in front of the TV. But Dad says we still have to eat at the table, not in front of the TV!

Now listen again.

18 *You will hear a boy talking about an accident he had. What has he hurt?*

Boy: The other bike came round the corner really fast and just crashed right into me! I'm lucky it wasn't more serious. I fell off my bike, but I didn't hit my head at all. I could get up and walk, no problem. But these three fingers hurt and I can't hold a pencil.

Now listen again.

19 *You will hear two teachers talking about an activity. What activity are they talking about?*

Teacher 1: That was good.
Teacher 2: It really was. If the boys start first and then the girls join in at the end of the first line, I think they'll sound great.
Teacher 1: They look good too, in their dark blue shirts and trousers.
Teacher 2: Yes, they do.

Now listen again.

20 *You will hear a girl who is unhappy with her food in a restaurant. What is the problem?*

Girl: Waiter! I'm sorry, I can't eat this.
Waiter: I'm sorry to hear that. Most people are very happy with the curry.
Girl: There's nothing wrong with the taste, but it's just room temperature.

Waiter: I'll bring you another one and I'll make sure it's hot this time.
Girl: Thank you.
Now listen again.
That is the end of Part 4.

Part 5

Track 19

Now look at Part 5.
For each question, choose the correct answer.
Look at Questions 21–25 now.
You have 15 seconds.
You will hear two parents talking about tidying the house.
Which part of the house will each child tidy?

Mother: All the children are home today, so let's get them to clean up!
Father: I've already told Amy to tidy the garage because she's the one who's always in there, fixing her bike.
Mother: And those are Roger's toys on the grass under the tree. He should pick them up.
Father: Right. Oh, look at all the dirty plates and glasses in here! Ruth is old enough to do the washing up. And Fiona can tidy in there. Her dolls are all over the sofa and it's impossible to sit anywhere.
Mother: And Chris did his homework at the table today and if he doesn't tidy this room, we'll have to eat in the kitchen.
Father: Yes, but Ken's books are also on the table. Let Ken tidy up here. I've got a special job for Chris.
Mother: What's that?
Father: He came in yesterday, took off his boots, and left them in front of the door! Along with his school bag and his football kit! I want the house to look tidy when I come inside! He needs to tidy it all!

Now listen again.
That is the end of Part 5. You now have six minutes to write your answers on the answer sheet.
That is the end of the test.

TEST 3   SPEAKING

Part 1

Track 20

Examiner:	Good evening. Can I have your mark sheets, please? I'm Kyle Hayes. And this is Tina Day. What's your name, Candidate A?
Candidate A:	My name's Juan Garcia.
Examiner:	And what's your name, Candidate B?
[PAUSE FOR YOU TO ANSWER]	
Examiner:	Candidate B, how old are you?
[PAUSE FOR YOU TO ANSWER]	
Examiner:	Where do you live, Candidate B?
[PAUSE FOR YOU TO ANSWER]	
Examiner:	Thank you. Candidate A, how old are you?
Candidate A:	I'm thirteen too.
Examiner:	Where do you live?
Candidate A:	I live in Buenos Aires as well, but I'm from Cordoba.
Examiner:	Thank you. Now, let's talk about your homes. Candidate A, can you tell me about your home?
Candidate A:	Yes, I live in an apartment in a big block. You have to take a lift to go up to it. It's on the sixth floor.
Examiner:	What is it like inside?
Candidate A:	It isn't very big, but it's nice. There are two bedrooms, one for my parents and one for me and my brother.
Examiner:	Candidate B, can you tell me about your home?
[PAUSE FOR YOU TO ANSWER]	
Examiner:	What is it like inside, Candidate B?
[PAUSE FOR YOU TO ANSWER]	
Examiner:	Now, Candidate A, is there anything that you don't like about your home?
Candidate A:	I don't like being in an apartment block. It means I have to go down in the lift every time I want to go outside or play football. I'd like to have a garden.
Examiner:	Now, let's talk about reading. Candidate B, what kind of things do you read?
[PAUSE FOR YOU TO ANSWER]	
Examiner:	How often do you read, Candidate B?
[PAUSE FOR YOU TO ANSWER]	
Examiner:	Candidate A, what kind of things do you read?
Candidate A:	I read when I study, but I don't often read outside school.
Examiner:	Why don't you like reading?
Candidate A:	I prefer to watch things on television or on the internet. I don't think books are as interesting as watching and listening. Reading feels like work to me.
Examiner:	Now, Candidate B, please tell me about something you have read recently.
[PAUSE FOR YOU TO ANSWER]	
Examiner:	Thank you.

Part 2

Track 21

Examiner:	Now, in this part of the test you are going to talk together. Here are some pictures that show different places to eat. Do you like these different places to eat? Say why or why not. I'll say that again. Do you like these different places to eat? Say why or why not. All right? Now, talk together.
Candidate A:	In my opinion, a fast food restaurant is a good place to eat. What do you think?
[PAUSE FOR YOU TO ANSWER]	
Candidate A:	Do you mean like this restaurant on a boat?
[PAUSE FOR YOU TO ANSWER]	
Candidate A:	Yes, very much. It's fun to have a picnic. You can enjoy playing football outside, and then you can stop and eat for a bit, and then you can play some more.
[PAUSE FOR YOU TO ANSWER]	
Candidate A:	Where do you go?
[PAUSE FOR YOU TO ANSWER]	
Candidate A:	Yes, we also take a picnic to the beach sometimes. That's my favourite place. What's your opinion about eating at home?
[PAUSE FOR YOU TO ANSWER]	
Candidate A:	Yes, I like eating at home too, but it's nice to go somewhere else to eat sometimes.
Examiner:	Candidate A, would you like to eat at a restaurant on a boat?
Candidate A:	Yes, I think so.
Examiner:	Why?
Candidate A:	It looks interesting. You can look around and enjoy the view while you eat.
Examiner:	Candidate B, would you like to eat at a restaurant on a boat?
[PAUSE FOR YOU TO ANSWER]	
Examiner:	So, Candidate A, which of these places to eat do you like the best?

Candidate A:	I think the fast food restaurant is the best place to eat.
Examiner:	And you, Candidate B, which of these places to eat do you like the best?

[PAUSE FOR YOU TO ANSWER]

Examiner:	Thank you. Can I have the booklet, please?
Examiner:	Now, Candidate B, can you compare eating on a boat with eating inside at a nice restaurant?

[PAUSE FOR YOU TO ANSWER]

Examiner:	And what about you, Candidate A? Can you compare eating at a fast food restaurant to eating at a more expensive indoor restaurant?
Candidate A:	For me, eating at a fast food restaurant is better. I like food like burgers and French fries more than the kind of food they have in expensive restaurants. And you can wear jeans and a T-shirt, so it's more comfortable.
Examiner:	Candidate A, which of these places to eat is your least favourite?
Candidate A:	I think the expensive indoor restaurant is the worst.
Examiner:	Why?
Candidate A:	Well, as I said, it isn't very comfortable and I don't really like the food. Also, it takes a long time to eat a meal in an expensive restaurant and it's boring. I don't like sitting still and talking for a long time.
Examiner:	Which of these places to eat do you think is the worst, Candidate B?

[PAUSE FOR YOU TO ANSWER]

Examiner:	Thank you. That is the end of the test.

TEST 4   LISTENING

Part 1

Track 22

Key English Test for Schools, Listening.
There are five parts to the test. You will hear each piece twice.
We will now stop for a moment.
Please ask any questions now, because you must not speak during the test.
Now look at the instructions for Part 1.
For each question, choose the correct answer.
Look at Question 1.

1 *What time does school start today?*

Boy:	Hurry up, Mum! You said you'd give me a lift to school!
Mother:	We've got lots of time. School starts at eight thirty, doesn't it?

Boy:	Usually, but we've got sports day this afternoon, so we're starting at eight fifteen, and it takes fifteen minutes to get to school.
Mother:	Well, it's only seven forty-five now, so don't worry.

Now listen again.

2 *How is Flora going to talk to her grandmother?*

Mother:	Don't forget, Flora, we're talking to Granny tonight.
Flora:	Are we going to go online again?
Mother:	Well, Granny had problems with her laptop last time, but she's got a new mobile with a video chat app that she wants to try.
Flora:	Oh, good. I hate talking to her on the landline. I want to see her face when we talk.

Now listen again.

3 *Where does the girl want to stay?*

Boy:	Where do you want to stay when we go on holiday? I want to go camping.
Girl:	But we did that last time. Why don't we ever stay in a nice hotel?
Boy:	Mum doesn't like them. She wants to rent a small place in the countryside.
Girl:	What is there to do in a house in the countryside?

Now listen again.

4 *What is Richard going to do after school?*

Tina:	Are you coming to the beach this afternoon, Richard?
Richard:	Hi Tina! I didn't know you were going! I've got too much homework.
Tina:	The weekend starts tomorrow. Do it on Saturday.
Richard:	I can't. That's the day I tidy my room.
Tina:	But everybody's going to the beach.
Richard:	You're trying to get me into trouble. No, homework is top of my list!

Now listen again.

5 *How much do the clothes cost?*

Assistant:	So, the skirt and two blouses come to sixty-six pounds.
Girl:	But there's a sale on! Ten percent! I thought sixty pounds would be enough.
Assistant:	The sale doesn't include children's clothes, I'm afraid.
Girl:	I've only got sixty pounds. I'll have to put something back.

Now listen again.
That is the end of Part 1.

Part 2

Track 23

Now look at Part 2.
For each question, write the correct answer in the gap.
Write one word or a number or a date or a time. Look at
Questions 6–10 now.
You have ten seconds.
You will hear a teacher telling students about the new
school library.

Teacher:	OK, so I have some good news. You've all seen the building work that's been going on for a few months next to the gym. I'm pleased to say that you can start using the new library from Monday. It will open early every morning at quarter past eight, so you can go there before classes start if you want to. We have a new English teacher at the school this term and he'll be looking after the library, but he can't do it on his own. He needs students to help him at lunchtimes. If you can help, please see Mr Howell during the break. Howell is spelled H-O-W-E-L-L. Now, the top floor of the library is for students who need somewhere quiet to do their homework after school, and that part of the library will be open until six o'clock every evening, Monday to Friday. There'll be a short ceremony to open the library tomorrow after school for students and parents. Please come if you can and please invite your mums and dads too.

Now listen again.
That is the end of Part 2.

Part 3

Track 24

Now look at Part 3.
For each question, choose the correct answer. Look at
Questions 11–15 now. You have 20 seconds.
You will hear Astrid talking to Albert about her new
summer job.

Albert:	Hi Astrid. How's your summer job?
Astrid:	I only started on Saturday. It's too early to know if I'm going to enjoy it.
Albert:	Where is it?
Astrid:	In a flower shop. I clean up and throw the old flowers away. I'm learning to tell when the flowers are still fresh enough to sell and when to throw them in the rubbish. I don't know enough about the different kinds of flowers to talk to customers yet.
Albert:	What about your colleagues?
Astrid:	They're like me – young, and they want to have fun at work. There's Joni and Kylie, they're sisters, and another girl, Mary. Mrs Jones, the boss, is very friendly.
Albert:	Do you have to work every Saturday?
Astrid:	I work one Saturday every two weeks. Mrs Jones said that if I ask her a week before, I can change my work days, but only if another girl can work on the days I'm not working.
Albert:	So, you can come to the beach next Saturday!
Astrid:	Well, let me see about that. I've got a lot of things to do at the moment.

Now listen again.
That is the end of Part 3.

Part 4

Track 25

Now look at Part 4.
For each question, choose the correct answer.

16 *You will hear two friends talking. Why are they*
unhappy?

Girl:	What a terrible game!
Boy:	I know! The other team played well and we lost, but that wasn't the problem.
Girl:	I agree. I mean, winning is important, but playing well is more important.
Boy:	Yes. People should try at least. There was no reason to play like that!

Now listen again.

17 *You will hear a brother and sister talking. How is one*
of them going to travel?

Boy:	Have you got your ticket?
Girl:	Yes, I have.
Boy:	Passport?
Girl:	Yes. I'm ready. I feel sick!
Boy:	You'll be fine. I know you don't like flying, but it's much quicker than going by train. And the coach would take days!
Girl:	I know. I'll be OK.

Now listen again.

18 *You will hear a boy talking about his day. Where did*
he go?

Boy:	It was great. Everybody came, even Mike. I didn't know he was so good in the water – he swims like a fish and he's an excellent diver. We stayed in as long as we could, but in the end, we had to get out because there were some young kids coming for lessons.

Now listen again.

19 *You will hear a girl talking. What has she done?*

Girl:	What do you think? Do you like it? Is it too short? I took a photo with me to show what I wanted it to look like. But now I'm not sure if I like it or not. I wanted it to look nice for the party. And what am I going to wear?

Now listen again.

20 *You will hear a boy talking to his father about a camping trip. How long does he want to stay at the campsite?*

Boy:	We'd like to go on the fourth of March and stay until the ninth.
Father:	So five nights.
Boy:	Five? I thought it was six.
Father:	You arrive on Thursday the fourth and you're leaving on Tuesday the ninth, so you don't count that night.
Boy:	Oh yes, I see. Yes, that's right.

Now listen again.
That is the end of Part 4.

Part 5

Track 26

Now look at Part 5.
For each question, choose the correct answer.
Look at Questions 21–25 now.
You have 15 seconds.
You will hear two students talking about photographs for a school project. Who found the photographs of the animals?

Girl:	OK, let's see what photos we've got. Dennis looked for sea animals, right?
Boy:	No, he found North American animals, remember? Like this one of the bear catching the fish.
Girl:	So who found that photo?
Boy:	Elaine did.
Girl:	Amazing! Imagine seeing an animal this size while you're swimming! What other sea animals do we have?
Boy:	This dolphin jumping out of the water. I'd love to swim with one!
Girl:	Me too. Is that also Elaine's?
Boy:	No, that was Lucas. And look at the photo Mark found.
Girl:	What a beautiful big cat! Those black and yellow stripes and those yellow eyes! Imagine seeing it in the jungle! It's more beautiful than a lion.
Boy:	And Layla took this photo herself.
Girl:	Really? It's very good.
Boy:	She was at the zoo and she saw it jumping from tree to tree. It's got very long arms and legs, hasn't it?
Girl:	What did Karen find?
Boy:	Photos of desert animals. This one's my favourite. I'd love to ride one. They can travel for miles without drinking, you know.

Now listen again.
That is the end of Part 5. You now have six minutes to write your answers on the answer sheet.
That is the end of the test.

178

TEST 4   SPEAKING

Part 1

Track 27

Examiner:	Good morning. Can I have your mark sheets, please? I'm Lydia Miles. And this is Richard Molina. What's your name, Candidate A?
Candidate A:	My name's Yanjun Hu.
Examiner:	And what's your name, Candidate B?
[PAUSE FOR YOU TO ANSWER]	
Examiner:	Candidate B, how old are you?
[PAUSE FOR YOU TO ANSWER]	
Examiner:	Where do you come from, Candidate B?
[PAUSE FOR YOU TO ANSWER]	
Examiner:	Thank you. Candidate A, how old are you?
Candidate A:	I'm twelve.
Examiner:	Where are you from?
Candidate A:	I'm from Shanghai in China.
Examiner:	Thank you.
Examiner:	Now, let's talk about birthdays. Candidate A, do you usually do anything special on your birthday?
Candidate A:	Yes, I do. We usually go to a restaurant on my birthday to have a big meal.
Examiner:	Who goes to the restaurant?
Candidate A:	My parents and my grandparents come and I also invite some of my friends.
Examiner:	Candidate B, do you usually do anything special on your birthday?
[PAUSE FOR YOU TO ANSWER]	
Examiner:	Do you get presents on your birthday, Candidate B?
[PAUSE FOR YOU TO ANSWER]	
Examiner:	Now, Candidate A, please tell me about your last birthday.
Candidate A:	I was at home in Shanghai and it was a school day, so I went to school. The class sang 'Happy Birthday' to me. Then after school, we went to my favourite restaurant to celebrate. We stayed at the restaurant for a long time. It was a great day.
Examiner:	Now, let's talk about musical instruments. Candidate B, do you play any musical instruments?
[PAUSE FOR YOU TO ANSWER]	
Examiner:	What kind of things do you play, Candidate B?
[PAUSE FOR YOU TO ANSWER]	
Examiner:	Candidate A, do you play a musical instrument?

Candidate A:	Yes, I play the piano. My parents wanted me to learn and I started when I was in primary school.
Examiner:	What kind of music do you play?
Candidate A:	I play classical music because that's what my parents wanted me to do, but actually, I haven't played very much over the last year.
Examiner:	Now, Candidate B, what musical instrument would you like to play well?

[PAUSE FOR YOU TO ANSWER]

| Examiner: | Thank you. |

Part 2

Track 28

Examiner:	Now, in this part of the test you are going to talk together.
	Here are some pictures that show different school clubs.
	Do you like these different school clubs? Say why or why not. I'll say that again.
	Do you like these different school clubs? Say why or why not.
	All right? Now, talk together.
Candidate A:	I think the chess club is a good one to join. Do you agree?

[PAUSE FOR YOU TO ANSWER]

| Candidate A: | Yes, I do. It's a popular club in my school in China, but I didn't join it. What do you think about the computer club? |

[PAUSE FOR YOU TO ANSWER]

| Candidate A: | No, I don't think so. I think the same as you. What about cooking? |

[PAUSE FOR YOU TO ANSWER]

| Candidate A: | Yes, I think it's a good club to join. I can't cook anything either. Would you like to go to the dance club? |

[PAUSE FOR YOU TO ANSWER]

| Candidate A: | Yes, it's fun and I'd like to learn to dance well. I think going to a dance club is a good way to meet other people and you can keep fit. |

[PAUSE FOR YOU TO ANSWER]

Candidate A:	Yes, of course! You are right about that.
Examiner:	Candidate A, would you like to join a singing club?
Candidate A:	No, I wouldn't.
Examiner:	Why not?
Candidate A:	I'm terrible at singing and I think people would laugh at me if I went there. I don't think they'd let me join!
Examiner:	Candidate B, would you like to join a singing club?

[PAUSE FOR YOU TO ANSWER]

Examiner:	So, Candidate A, which of these school clubs do you like the best?
Candidate A:	I think the dance club is the best. If you go with your friends, you can have a lot of fun.
Examiner:	And you, Candidate B, which of these school clubs do you like the best?

[PAUSE FOR YOU TO ANSWER]

| Examiner: | Thank you. Can I have the booklet, please? |
| Examiner: | Now, Candidate B, can you compare the chess club with the computer club? |

[PAUSE FOR YOU TO ANSWER]

Examiner:	And what about you, Candidate A? Can you compare the singing club and the dance club?
Candidate A:	I also think these clubs are similar. They're for people who like to be active. But I think singing is a group activity. If you sing in a group, people can't hear just you, but when you dance, everybody can see you dancing.
Examiner:	Candidate A, which of these school clubs do you think is the worst?
Candidate A:	I think the computer club is the worst.
Examiner:	Why?
Candidate A:	I'm not interested in computers. I only use them for school work. I'm not interested in learning about them.
Examiner:	Which of these clubs do you think is the worst, Candidate B?

[PAUSE FOR YOU TO ANSWER]

| Examiner: | Thank you. That is the end of the test. |

TEST 5   LISTENING

Part 1

Track 29

Key English Test for Schools, Listening.
There are five parts to the test. You will hear each piece twice.
We will now stop for a moment.
Please ask any questions now, because you must not speak during the test.
Now look at the instructions for Part 1.
For each question, choose the correct answer.
Look at Question 1.

1 *What is the girl going to buy?*

Girl:	Mum and I are going shopping this afternoon.
Boy:	What for?
Girl:	The keyboard for my computer is broken, but that's not the only problem. The whole thing is really old, so Mum's going to buy

me one that's easy to carry. Then I can take it to school with me.

Boy: Nice.

Girl: I know. I can't wait.

Now listen again.

2 *Where does Joe live?*

Kay: Hi Joe! How's the new place?

Joe: Hi Kay. It's fantastic, better than the city.

Kay: Some people don't like living in an apartment.

Joe: I know, but my parents say it's cheap and it's near school.

Kay: Don't you miss your house near the sea?

Joe: A little, but I can get to the beach easily when I want to.

Now listen again.

3 *What did Susan eat?*

Mother: Would you like to eat something, Hugo? There are a few bananas and apples in the kitchen.

Hugo: Are there any strawberries?

Mother: Susan finished them all, but I'll get some more tomorrow when I go to the market.

Hugo: That's a good idea. Then I suppose I'll have an apple.

Now listen again.

4 *What is the girl going to wear to the party?*

Girl 1:   What shall I wear to the party?

Girl 2:   What about your dress with the flowers?

Girl 1:   I think everybody else will be in jeans.

Girl 2:   So wear jeans.

Girl 1:   But I want to wear something nice! I wear jeans every day.

Girl 2:   What about a skirt and blouse?

Girl 1:   Good idea. I wear jeans and my dress all the time.

Now listen again.

5 *How did Kenji get to the hospital?*

Mother: Hi Jack. Where's Kenji?

Jack: In hospital.

Mother: What happened?

Jack: He broke his finger.

Mother: Oh no! Rugby's such a rough sport!

Jack: They wanted to call an ambulance, but Kenji wouldn't let them.

Mother: Do you get an ambulance for a broken finger?

Jack: I don't know. He wanted to take his motorbike, but in the end, Mr Hendricks drove him there.

Now listen again.
That is the end of Part 1.

Part 2

Track 30

Now look at Part 2.
For each question, write the correct answer in the gap.
Write one word or a number or a date or a time. Look at Questions 6–10 now.
You have ten seconds.
You will hear a teacher talking about Sports Day.

Teacher: All right, as you know, it's Sports Day on Friday, so don't go to your classrooms first thing in the morning, like you usually do. Go straight to the gym. Please don't be late. I'll take your names to make sure you're all here. Sports Day will start at quarter to nine exactly and Mr Challis will give a short talk. Football fans will know that Ben Challis, that's C-H-A-L-L-I-S, is a great football player, and he was a student at this school fifteen years ago. After the talk, the sporting events will start. At the end of the day, there will be a walking race and we want everybody to take part in it. It starts at two forty-five. Please remember to bring some money with you to spend on food and drinks. All the money we make will be used to buy new equipment for the gym. We're going to try to raise seven hundred and fifty pounds by the end of the day.

Now listen again.
That is the end of Part 2.

Part 3

Track 31

Now look at Part 3.
For each question, choose the correct answer. Look at Questions 11–15 now. You have 20 seconds.
You will hear Charlie talking to Stephanie about his holiday.

Stephanie: Hi Charlie. How was Africa?

Charlie: Amazing! The best thing was seeing wild animals in the countryside where they live, in nature. So much better than seeing them in a zoo.

Stephanie: Where did you stay?

Charlie: We did some camping, which was great, but that was only two nights, and the rest of the time we stayed in a hotel. It was quite nice.

Stephanie: Was it hot?

Charlie: Yes. The sun is strong and you have to be careful how long you spend in the sun. We had to cover our arms and legs and wear a hat. But if you do that, you don't have to stay inside.

Stephanie: How was the food?

| Charlie: | Good, but there was too much meat. It was nice, but I don't eat it very much at home, so I missed having vegetables. How was your holiday? |
| Stephanie: | We had a beach holiday. The weather was better than we thought it would be, but our hotel was on a busy road, so it was difficult to sleep because we could hear cars all night. |

Now listen again.
That is the end of Part 3.

Part 4

Track 32

Now look at Part 4.
For each question, choose the correct answer.

16 *You will hear a girl talking to her friend. Why is she going home?*

Boy:	Hi Debbie. Where are you going?
Girl:	Home.
Boy:	Are you OK?
Girl:	I stayed up all night to finish my project. I've just given it to the teacher. So, I'm going to bed for a bit. I think I'll feel fine after I get a bit of rest.

Now listen again.

17 *You will hear a girl in a restaurant. What will she have to eat?*

Waiter:	Are you ready to order?
Girl:	Erm, does the chicken come with chips?
Waiter:	No, it comes with a salad, but you can order chips as well.
Girl:	I think that will be too much. I'll have the chicken as it comes, thank you.

Now listen again.

18 *You will hear a boy talking about something he did. Where did he go?*

| Boy: | It's a pity you didn't come with us! It was really good. We had great seats near the front, so we were close to them. It was such a good show and the lights were amazing! They played all their best songs and we sang along. |

Now listen again.

19 *You will hear a girl talking to a friend. What has she bought?*

Girl 1:	Look what I bought!
Girl 2:	Ooh! That looks expensive.
Girl 1:	It is.
Girl 2:	Why do you need one when you can take pictures with your phone?
Girl 1:	Because this takes much better ones. Then I can put them on my laptop and change them and make them look even better, how I want them.
Girl 2:	Oh, OK.

Now listen again.

20 *You will hear a boy describing an accident. What has he hurt?*

| Boy: | I was playing football and I was in goal. Then Andy kicked the ball really hard and I put out my arm to stop it. It hit my middle finger – look at the size of it now. It really hurts, but it's on my left hand, and I write with my right, so that's all right. |

Now listen again.
That is the end of Part 4.

Part 5

Track 33

Now look at Part 5.
For each question, choose the correct answer.
Look at Questions 21–25 now.
You have 15 seconds.
You will hear a brother and sister talking about family members who are coming to visit. How will each person travel?

Girl:	When is Aunt Edna arriving?
Boy:	Soon, I hope! She's bringing a cake. She told Mum she ordered her taxi for three o'clock and it's half past now. And it's only a thirty-minute journey.
Girl:	And why isn't Erin here yet? It only takes a few minutes from her place by bike.
Boy:	She got a flat tyre this morning and she hasn't fixed it yet, so she's walking.
Girl:	Oh, but Harry wanted to see her new bike and ride here with her.
Boy:	Well, he's going to arrive last. He's got a long way to come on two wheels!
Girl:	Talking about a long way, is Uncle Tony driving down? He's got a new sports car.
Boy:	He said he didn't fancy driving all the way from Scotland, so he's flying down.
Girl:	I hope Fred comes. We haven't seen him for ages.
Boy:	He told Mum he'll be at the railway station a little after four.
Girl:	Aunt Amy usually comes in a taxi, doesn't she? I wonder what time she'll be here.
Boy:	She's driving herself these days. It'll be great to see everybody.

Now listen again.
That is the end of Part 5. You now have six minutes to write your answers on the answer sheet.
That is the end of the test.

TEST 5   SPEAKING

Part 1

Track 34

Examiner:	Good afternoon. Can I have your mark sheets, please? I'm Michael Bates. And this is Rose Shipton. What's your name, Candidate A?
Candidate A:	My name's Laszlo Nagy.
Examiner:	And what's your name, Candidate B?
[PAUSE FOR YOU TO ANSWER]	
Examiner:	Candidate B, how old are you?
[PAUSE FOR YOU TO ANSWER]	
Examiner:	Where do you live, Candidate B?
[PAUSE FOR YOU TO ANSWER]	
Examiner:	Thank you. Candidate A, how old are you?
Candidate A:	I'm twelve too.
Examiner:	Where do you live?
Candidate A:	I also live in Budapest.
Examiner:	Thank you.
Examiner:	Now, let's talk about travel. Candidate A, do you often travel to other countries?
Candidate A:	Yes, I do. My parents like to go to new places and during the school holidays, we often travel outside Hungary.
Examiner:	Where was the last place you went to outside Hungary?
Candidate A:	The last time we travelled outside Hungary, we went to Croatia and spent two weeks at the seaside there.
Examiner:	Candidate B, do you often travel to other countries?
[PAUSE FOR YOU TO ANSWER]	
Examiner:	Can you tell me about the last time you travelled, Candidate B?
[PAUSE FOR YOU TO ANSWER]	
Examiner:	Now, Candidate A, please tell me about a place you would like to travel to.
Candidate A:	I'd love to travel to the USA and visit Los Angeles and California. I like watching American films and I'd like to see the places where they make the films.
Examiner:	Now, let's talk about brothers and sisters. Candidate B, do you have any brothers and sisters?
[PAUSE FOR YOU TO ANSWER]	
Examiner:	What's he like, Candidate B?
[PAUSE FOR YOU TO ANSWER]	
Examiner:	Candidate A, do you have any brothers and sisters?
Candidate A:	Yes, I have a brother and a sister.

Examiner:	What are they like?
Candidate A:	They're very nice. They're older than me and they help me with my homework.
Examiner:	Now, Candidate B, what is the best thing about having a brother?
[PAUSE FOR YOU TO ANSWER]	
Examiner:	Thank you.

Part 2

Track 35

Examiner:	Now, in this part of the test you are going to talk together. Here are some pictures that show different presents for people who have just got married. Do you like these different presents for people who have just got married? Say why or why not. I'll say that again. Do you like these different presents for people who have just got married? Say why or why not. All right? Now, talk together.
Candidate A:	This first picture is a clock. It's a beautiful clock and I think it's also a useful present to give people who have just got married. What do you think?
[PAUSE FOR YOU TO ANSWER]	
Candidate A:	It looks like a little table for the living room where you put things like magazines or glasses. I think it's called a coffee table. When people get married, they often need furniture, so it's another useful present.
[PAUSE FOR YOU TO ANSWER]	
Candidate A:	Yes, you could, but you could have it in another part of the house where everybody can see it, for example in the living room or the hall.
[PAUSE FOR YOU TO ANSWER]	
Candidate A:	Then there are these glasses. What do you think of them?
[PAUSE FOR YOU TO ANSWER]	
Candidate A:	Yes, I think you're right. The last present is money.
[PAUSE FOR YOU TO ANSWER]	
Candidate A:	But if you give people money, they know exactly how much you're giving them!
Examiner:	Candidate A, would you like somebody to give you money if you got married?
Candidate A:	I think so, yes.
Examiner:	Why?
Candidate A:	If somebody gives you money, you can buy what you want. Sometimes when

people get married, they might get two presents that are the same!

Examiner: Candidate B, would you like somebody to give you money if you got married?

[PAUSE FOR YOU TO ANSWER]

Examiner: So, Candidate A, which of these wedding presents do you like the best?

Candidate A: I think a mirror is the best because it's the most useful. Everybody can use a mirror.

Examiner: And you, Candidate B, which of these wedding presents do you like the best?

[PAUSE FOR YOU TO ANSWER]

Examiner: Thank you. Can I have the booklet, please?
Now, Candidate B, can you compare the clock with the glasses?

[PAUSE FOR YOU TO ANSWER]

Examiner: And what about you, Candidate A? Can you compare the coffee table with the mirror?

Candidate A: I think they're both good presents. You have to be careful with a mirror because it can break, and if you break one, you'll have bad luck! I don't think you can break a table easily. But you should be careful when you put something on it because you might make a mark on it.

Examiner: Candidate A, which of these presents do you think is the worst?

Candidate A: I think the glasses are the worst present.

Examiner: Why?

Candidate A: I don't think they're interesting.

Examiner: Which of these wedding presents do you think is the worst, Candidate B?

[PAUSE FOR YOU TO ANSWER]

Examiner: Thank you. That is the end of the test.

TEST 6   LISTENING

Part 1

Track 36

Key English Test for Schools, Listening.
There are five parts to the test. You will hear each piece twice.
We will now stop for a moment.
Please ask any questions now, because you must not speak during the test.
Now look at the instructions for Part 1.
For each question, choose the correct answer.
Look at Question 1.

1 *Who is Uncle Frank?*

Boy: These are nice photos. Is that your Uncle Frank?

Girl: Uncle Frank doesn't wear glasses! Don't you remember?

Boy: No, I don't. I only saw him once three years ago. Is he that one?

Girl: You have a terrible memory! He doesn't wear jackets like that! He always looks very smart. This one is Uncle Frank.

Now listen again.

2 *What time will the girl's father give her a lift home?*

Girl: Dad, can you pick me up after the film this afternoon?

Father: Hmm. What time?

Girl: The film finishes at quarter to four.

Father: Well, I can't leave work until four and I need quarter of an hour to get to the cinema.

Girl: OK, that's fine. I can find something to do for thirty minutes.

Now listen again.

3 *What job is Jason doing this summer?*

Maria: Are you washing cars again this summer, Jason?

Jason: I wanted to, but they didn't need me this year, so my brother got me a job three days a week at the farm where he's working.

Maria: I thought he was a window cleaner.

Jason: He isn't doing that anymore, but I wouldn't mind cleaning windows next summer.

Now listen again.

4 *Which dog is Michael's?*

Vicky: Hi Michael. How's your new dog?

Michael: Hi Vicky. He's lovely. His name's Benji.

Vicky: What's he like?

Michael: Well, he isn't a small dog like yours. He's quite big. Yours has long hair, hasn't he? Don't you have to brush it a lot?

Vicky: Yes, all the time.

Michael: Well, we don't have to worry about that with Benji.

Now listen again.

5 *Where does Mary want to put the food for the party?*

Mary: I'm going to put the food in the dining room, Mum.

Mother: Oh. Is that a good idea? Isn't it better in the kitchen? It'll be easier to clean up afterwards.

Mary: It's too far from the party room, and if it's nice, we'll be in the garden.

Mother: Can't you put the food out there?

Mary: It might rain.

Now listen again.
That is the end of Part 1.

Part 2

Track 37

Now look at Part 2.
For each question, write the correct answer in the gap.
Write one word or a number or a date or a time. Look at
Questions 6–10 now.
You have ten seconds.
You will hear a teacher talking about the school play.

Teacher: Good afternoon everybody. Please be quiet and listen carefully. I have some information about this year's school play: *A Happy House.* It's a great play with parts for many actors, so if you're interested in being in it, please contact Mrs Kearnes, the English teacher. It's best to email her. That's Mrs Rita Kearnes. That's K-E-A-R-N-E-S. We're very lucky this year. We usually have the school play in the school hall, but this year we can use a real theatre in the city centre. That means we can sell many more tickets because it's got one thousand three hundred seats. It's going to be a very special event, so please come if you can and bring your parents and friends. Tickets for adults cost £5, for children aged 11 to 16 they're £3, and for children under 10 years they're just £1. The date of the play is the fourteenth of March.

Now listen again.
That is the end of Part 2.

Part 3

Track 38

Now look at Part 3.
For each question, choose the correct answer. Look at
Questions 11–15 now. You have 20 seconds.
You will hear Amna talking to Farhan about a concert.

Farhan: Hi Amna. Where have you been?
Amna: To a concert with Yasmin.
Farhan: How was it?
Amna: Great. I didn't really know what it would be like. Yasmin loves that band, Loud Girls, she's such a big fan, and she asked me to go with her. I don't usually like pop music, but I'm glad I went.
Farhan: Did you have good seats?
Amna: Yes, in the end. At first, we were behind some really tall boys and we couldn't see well, but we moved to two empty seats near the front.
Farhan: Did they play any good songs?
Amna: Yes. They were fantastic and the music wasn't too loud. You know when it's so loud you can't talk to anybody? I hate that. Unfortunately, we missed the last bus back home and we had to walk to the railway station. We couldn't get a taxi. Do you ever go to concerts?

Farhan: All the time, but Loud Girls isn't my sort of thing, I prefer rock music.
Now listen again.
That is the end of Part 3.

Part 4

Track 39

Now look at Part 4.
For each question, choose the correct answer.

16 *You will hear a father talking to his son. What does he want his son to do?*

Father: Look at this place! Will you tidy up in here, please?
Boy: Why me?
Father: Your sister is doing the kitchen, and all the things in here are yours. Look, your magazines, there, on the sofa! Your games on the floor in front of the TV! We've got guests coming soon and we want to sit in here. I'll do the bathroom.

Now listen again.

17 *You will hear a girl talking. Why does she feel bad?*

Girl: I feel terrible. I didn't get to bed until really late because I stayed up watching a horror film. I'm not tired – I often go to bed late and I don't need much sleep. It's my stomach. I think it must have been the curry I had.

Now listen again.

18 *You will hear Skye talking to her dad. Where are they?*

Dad: Do you like the chair, Skye?
Skye: I love it!
Dad: How about putting it next to the window? Then we can sit there and read or look outside.
Skye: It's going to be a lovely surprise for Mum. Now we've got enough chairs when Granny and Grandad come for a visit ... What are we having for dinner?

Now listen again.

19 *You will hear a man talking about his day. What is his job?*

Man: What a day! First, I had to take the children to school. Tommy forgot his lunch, so we had to go back home for it. Then I was in meetings all day. I missed my doctor's appointment, but I made a new one with the nurse. Tomorrow I have to explain to my boss why I'm not selling enough.

Now listen again.

20 *You will hear two students talking about a school club. Which club have they been to?*

Student 1: That was fun! Did you see what Emma made?
Student 2: It didn't look very good, did it?
Student 1: No, but it was delicious!

Student 2:	I'm going to have mine when I get home. But I want to take a picture of it before I have it. Then tomorrow I have to go for a long bike ride to work it all off!

Now listen again.
That is the end of Part 4.

Part 5

Track 40

Now look at Part 5.
For each question, choose the correct answer.
Look at Questions 21–25 now.
You have 15 seconds.
You will hear two parents talking about the new school year. What do their children need?

Woman:	We really must go shopping for the children!
Man:	I know! Julia says she can't walk because her shoes are too small. She says she's seen a pair she likes.
Woman:	Paul needs a bigger bag for all his books this year. Something big enough for his sports clothes as well.
Man:	OK. Mickey says he needs a lot of stuff for art club and you know what he's like – if he doesn't have it, he'll say Tatum's pictures are better than his because she's got better things!
Woman:	True ... Now it's getting colder, Tatum needs something to wear over her jumper. She hasn't said anything to me, but I know she needs it.
Man:	What about Zoe?
Woman:	We gave her lots of presents on her birthday, including a new watch, so she doesn't need anything like that. But I must take her to have her eyes tested before school starts. She says she can't read what's on the board.
Man:	Linda is the problem. She needs all the kit for her new school: new skirts, new shirts, new jumpers ...

Now listen again.
That is the end of Part 5. You now have six minutes to write your answers on the answer sheet.
That is the end of the test.

TEST 6   SPEAKING

Part 1

Track 41

Examiner:	Good evening. Can I have your mark sheets, please? I'm Theresa Wood. And this is David Stillwell. What's your name, Candidate A?

Candidate A:	My name's Margarita Lopez.
Examiner:	And what's your name, Candidate B?
[PAUSE FOR YOU TO ANSWER]	
Examiner:	Candidate B, how old are you?
[PAUSE FOR YOU TO ANSWER]	
Examiner:	Where are you from, Candidate B?
[PAUSE FOR YOU TO ANSWER]	
Examiner:	Thank you. Candidate A, how old are you?
Candidate A:	I'm thirteen.
Examiner:	Where are you from?
Candidate A:	I'm from Mexico.
Examiner:	Thank you.
Examiner:	Now, let's talk about keeping fit. Candidate A, what do you do to keep fit?
Candidate A:	I play lots of sport. I play basketball and badminton.
Examiner:	Where do you play them?
Candidate A:	I play basketball at school and I play badminton at home with my sister.
Examiner:	Candidate B, what do you do to keep fit?
[PAUSE FOR YOU TO ANSWER]	
Examiner:	What do you like so much about that sport, Candidate B?
[PAUSE FOR YOU TO ANSWER]	
Examiner:	Now Candidate A, do you think it is important to keep fit?
Candidate A:	Yes, I do.
Examiner:	Why?
Candidate A:	I don't want to put on weight or be unhealthy. If you're fit, you feel good and you're happy. You do better in life and you enjoy more activities.
Examiner:	Now, let's talk about exams at school. Candidate B, how do you feel about school exams?
[PAUSE FOR YOU TO ANSWER]	
Examiner:	Why not, Candidate B?
[PAUSE FOR YOU TO ANSWER]	
Examiner:	Candidate A, how do you feel about school exams?
Candidate A:	Exams are OK for me.
Examiner:	Aren't they hard?
Candidate A:	They aren't too hard and my parents don't worry too much about my marks. They help me, they want me to do well, but they don't get upset if I get a bad mark.
Examiner:	Now, Candidate B, can you tell me about an exam where you did very well or badly?
[PAUSE FOR YOU TO ANSWER]	
Examiner:	Thank you.

Part 2

Track 42

Examiner:	Now, in this part of the test you are going to talk together. Here are some pictures that show different family days out. Do you like these different family days out? Say why or why not. I'll say that again. Do you like these different family days out? Say why or why not. All right? Now, talk together.
Candidate A:	The first day out is a trip to the zoo. I think it's quite a good day out. Do you agree?
[PAUSE FOR YOU TO ANSWER]	
Candidate A:	It might be good, if it's an interesting museum, but some museums are boring.
[PAUSE FOR YOU TO ANSWER]	
Candidate A:	The next one is a shopping centre. We often go to one with my family. In my opinion, it's a good way to spend the day. You can buy some new clothes and you can have something to eat there as well.
[PAUSE FOR YOU TO ANSWER]	
Candidate A:	What about going to the park? I think that's a good day out, especially if the children are young.
[PAUSE FOR YOU TO ANSWER]	
Candidate A:	And finally, the water park. I think the water park is great. It's a really good day out for the family.
[PAUSE FOR YOU TO ANSWER]	
Examiner:	Candidate A, you said the water park is great. Why do you say that?
Candidate A:	There are different things you can do. You can go for a swim, you can lie in the sun, and, of course, there are slides. Some of them are really big and you can go down them really fast. It's exciting.
Examiner:	Candidate B, you said young children can do whatever they like in the park. What sort of things do children do in a park?
[PAUSE FOR YOU TO ANSWER]	
Examiner:	So, Candidate A, which of these family days out do you like the best?
Candidate A:	I think the water park is the best day out.
Examiner:	And you, Candidate B, which of these days out do you think is the best?
[PAUSE FOR YOU TO ANSWER]	

Examiner:	Thank you. Can I have the booklet, please?
Examiner:	Now, Candidate B, can you compare going to the zoo with going to the museum?
[PAUSE FOR YOU TO ANSWER]	
Examiner:	And what about you, Candidate A? Can you compare going to a shopping centre with going to the zoo?
Candidate A:	They're very different activities. If you go to a zoo, you see nature, but a shopping centre is nothing like nature. It's indoors and you don't get any fresh air. But if the weather is bad or if it's too hot outside, a shopping centre can be comfortable.
Examiner:	Candidate A, which of these days out do you think is the worst?
Candidate A:	I think the museum is the worst.
Examiner:	Why?
Candidate A:	Museums are usually full of old things and most of them are boring.
Examiner:	Which of these days out do you think is the worst, Candidate B?
[PAUSE FOR YOU TO ANSWER]	
Examiner:	Thank you. That is the end of the test.

TEST 7   LISTENING

Part 1

Track 43

Key English Test for Schools, Listening.
There are five parts to the test. You will hear each piece twice.
We will now stop for a moment.
Please ask any questions now, because you must not speak during the test.
Now look at the instructions for Part 1.
For each question, choose the correct answer.
Look at Question 1.

1 *What pet will the children get?*

Girl:	We should get another pet.
Boy:	I know. Goldie is nice, but you can't play with a fish.
Girl:	I'd love a dog. You can do lots of things with dogs.
Boy:	But you have to take them for walks. Cats are easier to look after.
Girl:	But it might try to eat the fish.
Boy:	I didn't think of that. OK, you win.
Now listen again.	

2 *Where is Polly's ruler?*

Mother:	Hurry up, Polly! You'll be late for school.
Polly:	I'm looking for my ruler!

Mother:	I saw it in your room.
Polly:	Where? I can't find it!
Mother:	On your desk. By your books. Next to your mug with all your pens and pencils in it.
Polly:	Oh yes.

Now listen again.

3 *What will the boy take to the picnic?*

Girl:	What are you going to take to the picnic?
Boy:	Just some things to drink out of.
Girl:	Is that all!?
Boy:	Kevin's bringing everything else. The food, drinks and plates. He's got everything except cups.

Now listen again.

4 *What has Larry got?*

Meg:	Hey, Larry! How did you get here?
Larry:	Hi Meg. I got here on my new wheels.
Meg:	But you haven't got enough money for a car.
Larry:	Who needs a car? Look outside!
Meg:	Wow! Can you take me for a ride on it?
Larry:	When I've passed my test, but not until then.
Meg:	It looks really fast.

Now listen again.

5 *What shoes does the girl want?*

Girl:	Mum, can you buy me some new shoes?
Mother:	No, your school shoes are fine.
Girl:	I don't mean for school. I mean these ones in the magazine.
Mother:	They're nice, but when are you going to wear them? You always wear trainers.
Girl:	Well, I want something different, and these are so pretty. Please, Mum.

Now listen again.
That is the end of Part 1.

Part 2

Track 44

Now look at Part 2.
For each question, write the correct answer in the gap.
Write one word or a number or a date or a time. Look at Questions 6–10 now.
You have ten seconds.
You will hear a student giving a talk about the longest bridge in the world.

Student:	Today I'm going to talk about the Danyang-Kunshan Grand Bridge in China. It's the longest bridge in the world: 169 kilometres long! The bridge is on the railway line between two large cities, Shanghai and Nanjing. It's a rail bridge, which means trains use it. You can't drive or walk over

it. It's in the Jiangsu area of China. Let me spell Jiangsu for you: J-I-A-N-G-S-U. They finished building the bridge in 2010, but it was only opened a year later, in 2011. More than ten thousand workers worked on it and it took four years to build. It goes over fields where rice is grown, rivers and a lake. Actually, if you look at a list of the longest bridges in the world, most of them are in China. Danyang-Kunshan Grand Bridge is also one of the most expensive bridges in the world. China also has the world's longest and highest bridge made of glass. It was built to attract tourists!

Now listen again.
That is the end of Part 2.

Part 3

Track 45

Now look at Part 3.
For each question, choose the correct answer. Look at Questions 11–15 now. You have 20 seconds.
You will hear Trevor talking to Melanie about a visit to a museum.

Melanie:	Hi Trevor. How was the museum?
Trevor:	Fantastic. Have you been yet, Melanie?
Melanie:	No, and I'm not even sure where it is.
Trevor:	Well, it's only been open a few days. It's on the corner of Baker Street and Third Street, where the old cinema used to be. Across the road from the library.
Melanie:	Oh!
Trevor:	Most of the time I don't find museums interesting – I really don't need to see any more dinosaurs! But this is a science museum.
Melanie:	What did you see?
Trevor:	Lots of things. My favourite was the planetarium.
Melanie:	What's that?
Trevor:	It's a large room without windows. You sit down and the seats go back. Then they turn off the lights, so it's dark, and then suddenly you see thousands of lights on the ceiling: all the stars in the sky.
Melanie:	Were there lots of people?
Trevor:	I thought there would be, but it was quiet and there weren't a lot of kids.
Melanie:	I'll go this weekend or the next.
Trevor:	It might be crowded on Saturdays and Sundays. I'd go another day if I were you.

Now listen again.
That is the end of Part 3.

187

Part 4

Track 46

Now look at Part 4.
For each question, choose the correct answer.

16 *You will hear two parents talking. Where are they?*

Mother: Oh no! It's started to rain.

Father: Oh bother! We've only just got here!

Mother: The children will be so disappointed. They wanted to go swimming. Let's wait a bit.

Father: Good idea. We can't even sit in the garden if it's raining. At least we didn't drive all the way to the mountains.

Now listen again.

17 *You will hear a boy talking about an evening at the cinema. What was the problem?*

Boy: At first, I didn't want to go because I thought it would be boring, but the story was good, and there was some great action. And this time people weren't talking all the time. But there were a couple of really tall men sitting in front of us and it was difficult to see the screen.

Now listen again.

18 *You will hear a brother and sister talking in a café. What is the girl going to have?*

Boy: Is that all you're having?

Girl: Yes, that's all.

Boy: I'm going to have a piece of chocolate cake. What about you?

Girl: I don't think so. A juice is more than enough. I'm still full from lunch. Mum's pasta was delicious.

Boy: Yes, it was good.

Now listen again.

19 *You will hear a head teacher talking to a student. What is the problem?*

Head teacher: Now Jack, your class teacher has asked me to talk to you. Mrs Evans is worried about you. You get to class on time now, so that's good, and your homework is also much better. But you have to stop chatting to other students during lessons. It means other children can't study properly – and you can't either.

Now listen again.

20 *You will hear a teacher talking in class. What subject does she teach?*

Teacher: So, your homework is to work on your pictures. You have to name the different parts of the plants. Explain why they need light from the sun and what happens when it's dark. You don't need to colour your pictures, but you need to write about 200 words.

Now listen again.
That is the end of Part 4.

Part 5

Track 47

Now look at Part 5.
For each question, choose the correct answer.
Look at Questions 21–25 now.
You have 15 seconds.
Two parents are looking through a cupboard full of things that belonged to their children a long time ago. Who did the things belong to?

Mother: Look at all these things! Aha! These are Max's. Remember how much he loved these stories about the baby rabbit when he was little!

Father: And look at these plastic rings and necklaces. Emma played with them all the time. She would even sleep with them on!

Mother: Oh, we've still got Alfie's drum kit! He didn't play on it much, did he? No. Once he started playing football, he stopped doing anything else.

Father: Thankfully! He made a terrible noise. Oh look! Baby shoes and a baby jumper. These were Daniel's. He was a sweet baby – and quiet.

Mother: And now look at him!

Father: Oh, here's a doll and a doll's house. These were Lea's, weren't they?

Mother: That doll? It was Jan's, and the doll's house was hers too. Lea preferred playing outside. Here's her little tent. She wanted to sleep in it in the garden, remember?

Father: Now, what are we going to do with all these things?

Now listen again.
That is the end of Part 5. You now have six minutes to write your answers on the answer sheet.
That is the end of the test.

TEST 7   SPEAKING

Part 1

Track 48

Examiner: Good morning.
Can I have your mark sheets, please?
I'm Owen Taylor. And this is Hilary Dunn.
What's your name, Candidate A?

Candidate A: My name's Filip Kohel.

Examiner: And what's your name, Candidate B?

[PAUSE FOR YOU TO ANSWER]

Examiner: Candidate B, how old are you?

[PAUSE FOR YOU TO ANSWER]

Examiner: Where do you live, Candidate B?

[PAUSE FOR YOU TO ANSWER]

Examiner: Thank you.
Candidate A, how old are you?

Candidate A: I'm thirteen.

Examiner:	Where do you live?
Candidate A:	I live in Prague, but I come from Brno.
Examiner:	Thank you. Now, let's talk about neighbours. Candidate A, what are your neighbours like?
Candidate A:	I live in a flat, so I have a lot of neighbours. I don't know them all, but the ones on our floor are very nice.
Examiner:	Can you tell me about the neighbours who live the closest to you?
Candidate A:	They're an old man and his wife. I know them well because sometimes they looked after me when I was small.
Examiner:	Candidate B, do you have neighbours?

[PAUSE FOR YOU TO ANSWER]

Examiner:	What are they like, Candidate B?

[PAUSE FOR YOU TO ANSWER]

Examiner:	Now, Candidate A, please tell me what you think makes a good neighbour.
Candidate A:	A good neighbour will help you if you have a problem, for example, if you need something. You can knock on their door, ask for what you need and they'll help you.
Examiner:	Now, let's talk about what sort of person you are. Candidate B, do you think you are a happy person?

[PAUSE FOR YOU TO ANSWER]

Examiner:	What makes you happy, Candidate B?

[PAUSE FOR YOU TO ANSWER]

Examiner:	Candidate A, what sort of person are you? Are you quiet or do you talk a lot?
Candidate A:	I think I talk a lot.
Examiner:	Who do you talk with and what about?
Candidate A:	I talk with my friends all the time. My teachers in school sometimes get angry because I talk too much in class.
Examiner:	Now, Candidate B, can you tell me what you do if you have had a bad day and you want to feel better?

[PAUSE FOR YOU TO ANSWER]

Examiner:	Thank you.

Part 2

Track 49

Examiner:	Now, in this part of the test you are going to talk together.
	Here are some pictures that show different jobs. Do you like these different jobs? Say why or why not. I'll say that again. Do you like these different jobs? Say why or why not. All right? Now, talk together.
Candidate A:	The first picture is somebody working in a library. Do you think that's a good job?

[PAUSE FOR YOU TO ANSWER]

Candidate A:	I don't think I'd like to work in a library, but it would be great for somebody who loves books and reading. What about being a doctor?

[PAUSE FOR YOU TO ANSWER]

Candidate A:	Yes, I agree with you. My parents would like me to be a doctor.

[PAUSE FOR YOU TO ANSWER]

Candidate A:	I don't know. I haven't thought about it before. Maybe you can get cheap clothes if you work in a shop!

[PAUSE FOR YOU TO ANSWER]

Candidate A:	Yes! You must be very good and you have to practise a lot. And the last picture is a business person. I'd love that job. What about you?

[PAUSE FOR YOU TO ANSWER]

Examiner:	Candidate A, why do you think being a business person is a good job?
Candidate A:	I think you can make a lot of money if you're good at it. You could start your own business, work hard and become rich.
Examiner:	Candidate B, you said you don't want to be a business person because it's hard work. Is there anything else you don't like about this job?

[PAUSE FOR YOU TO ANSWER]

Examiner:	So, Candidate A, which of these jobs do you like the best?
Candidate A:	I think a business person has the best job.
Examiner:	And you, Candidate B, which of these jobs do you like the best?

[PAUSE FOR YOU TO ANSWER]

Examiner:	Thank you. Can I have the booklet, please? Now, Candidate B, can you compare working in a library with working as a shop assistant?

[PAUSE FOR YOU TO ANSWER]

Examiner:	And what about you, Candidate A? Can you compare a musician with a doctor?
Candidate A:	In my opinion, they're both good jobs and they're both difficult. You have to spend a long time studying and practising before you can be a musician or a doctor. I think lots of

people would like to do these jobs, but only a few will be successful.

Examiner: Candidate A, which of these jobs are you least interested in doing?

Candidate A: I wouldn't be interested in working in a shop.

Examiner: Why not?

Candidate A: I think it's boring and very tiring.

Examiner: Which of these jobs are you least interested in, Candidate B?

[PAUSE FOR YOU TO ANSWER]

Examiner: Thank you. That is the end of the test.

TEST 8   LISTENING

Part 1

Track 50

Key English Test for Schools, Listening.
There are five parts to the test. You will hear each piece twice.
We will now stop for a moment.
Please ask any questions now, because you must not speak during the test.
Now look at the instructions for Part 1.
For each question, choose the correct answer.
Look at Question 1.

1 *What can't Mona find?*

Father: Are you ready, Mona? We have to leave for the airport now or we'll be late.

Mona: I can't find it!

Father: What?

Mona: How am I going to contact my friends without it?

Father: Oh. That.

Mona: Where did I put it? I've got my passport, I don't need my library card, so I'm leaving that … What am I going to do?

Now listen again.

2 *What days does Katie have to take the dog for a walk?*

Mother: You have to take the dog for a walk, Katie, because of my bad leg.

Katie: Every day?

Mother: No, not every day. Dad can do that on Monday because he gets home from work early, but you have to do the next three days. I think I'll be better on Friday, so I can probably do it then.

Katie: Oh, OK.

Now listen again.

3 *How will Jamie and Linda get to the park?*

Linda: Come on, Jamie! Let's go! The others are waiting for us at the park.

Jamie: Let's go by bike.

Linda: The bus will be quicker.

Jamie: But there's a lot of traffic today, Linda. Walking would be better than the bus if you don't want to cycle.

Linda: OK, let's do that, then. Cycling in town is scary.

Now listen again.

4 *What is David painting?*

Teacher: That's lovely, David!

David: Thank you. I started with the fruit, but it was difficult, so I got a new piece of paper and tried to paint the flowers. But they were even harder, so I went back to the fruit.

Teacher: What about the guitar?

David: It isn't as interesting to paint as flowers and fruit. I'll paint the guitar next time.

Now listen again.

5 *What will Tommy wear?*

Mother: It's cold out there! Wear something warm, Tommy. Put this coat on.

Tommy: Oh Mum! I'm not wearing that! People will laugh at me.

Mother: Well, wear the winter hat that your grandma made you. And the scarf and gloves.

Tommy: I'll wear the scarf and gloves, but the hat's too small.

Now listen again.
That is the end of Part 1.

Part 2

Track 51

Now look at Part 2.
For each question, write the correct answer in the gap.
Write one word or a number or a date or a time. Look at Questions 6–10 now.
You have ten seconds.
You will hear a school nurse talking to students at the beginning of the school year.

Nurse: Hello. I'm Mrs Jenkins, the school nurse. I hope you all stay well and healthy this year, but here's some information if you need it. Firstly, if you are ill in the morning before school, please stay at home! But if you feel ill at school, come and see me. My room is number 34, upstairs in the main building. I'm there from nine o'clock in the morning until three o'clock in the afternoon. If there's an emergency, and you or another student is seriously hurt or ill, call 999 immediately and then come and look for me. But please remember: I can try to help you, but I can't give you any medicine. If you need medicine, we'll arrange to take you to see a doctor. Also remember: I'm not only here if you're hurt or ill. I'm also here for you if you're unhappy about something, so don't be afraid to come to see me for any reason.

Now listen again.
That is the end of Part 2.

Part 3

Track 52

Now look at Part 3.
For each question, choose the correct answer. Look at Questions 11–15 now. You have 20 seconds.
You will hear Adriana talking to Felix about a bicycle ride she went on.

Felix: What did you do yesterday, Adriana?
Adriana: I went for a bicycle ride.
Felix: Who with?
Adriana: With my friend Mina. Joe and Carrie couldn't come, so it was just us. I'm not brave enough to go on my own.
Felix: Did you go far?
Adriana: I'm not sure how many kilometres we did. We cycled for three hours, but it wasn't a race! We went at a comfortable speed.
Felix: Where did you go?
Adriana: Well, Mina came to my place and we rode along the road to the forest. Then there's a small foot path which is just wide enough for cycling. It goes through the forest, across the fields and down to the sea.
Felix: Nice.
Adriana: When we came back, we took the road over the hills, so we did a circle and we didn't have to go on any main roads or come back the same way we went.
Felix: Did you have a picnic?
Adriana: Well, we decided to go cycling at the last minute. We didn't have time to make any sandwiches, so we had fish and chips by the sea.
Felix: Sounds great.
Now listen again.
That is the end of Part 3.

Part 4

Track 53

Now look at Part 4.
For each question, choose the correct answer.

16 *You will hear a girl talking. What does she need?*

Girl: It was such a stupid thing to happen! I sat down on the sofa to read my book and I felt something behind me and I heard it breaking! I jumped up, but it was too late. My trousers and jumper had glass on them. I need a new pair now – I can't read anything!
Now listen again.

17 *You will hear a brother and sister talking about a birthday present for their mother. What are they looking at?*

Girl: Do you think she'll like this?
Boy: Yes, I think so!
Girl: She said not to get her anything to eat …

Boy: Yes, she did. She loves chocolates, but she says she eats too many. And we've got flowers in the garden already.
Girl: Ooh, the smell is lovely! I think I'll start having baths instead of showers.
Now listen again.

18 *You will hear a mother talking to her child. Where are they?*

Mother: Did you like that? You looked like you were having fun. Now, get changed quickly or we're going to be late. Here's a towel and there are your clothes. Just make sure you're dry before you get dressed. Hurry. Daddy's waiting for us at home.
Now listen again.

19 *You will hear two students talking about somebody. Who are they talking about?*

Student 1: She's very nice, isn't she?
Student 2: She is. I didn't understand that maths, but she explained it really well.
Student 1: Better than the teacher!
Student 2: We should ask her to join our study group! Now, I've got to go. My mum's waiting for me!
Now listen again.

20 *You will hear two students talking. Where are they?*

Student 1: Have you got much homework?
Student 2: A little. I've done most of it, so I'm going to see a film later.
Student 1: Don't your parents mind when you go out on a school night?
Student 2: No, but I don't go out very often, and Thursday is nearly the weekend. OK, this is my stop. I'm getting off. See you tomorrow.
Now listen again.
That is the end of Part 4.

Part 5

Track 54

Now look at Part 5.
For each question, choose the correct answer.
Look at Questions 21–25 now.
You have 15 seconds.
You will hear two friends talking about a school holiday. Where do their friends want to go?

Girl: What does everybody want to do tomorrow?
Boy: Lisa wants to go to town for some summer clothes and a lamp for her bedroom.
Girl: She always wants to go shopping! Glen wants to see a play. One of his friends is in it.
Boy: Kim doesn't want to do that. She thinks plays are boring, but there's a film she wants to see.
Girl: Those are evening activities. What about during the day?
Boy: Haruko told me about a tree climbing experience you can do. He says the place is

great and you can also go on a nature walk through the trees.

Girl: There's a lake near there too, isn't there?

Boy: Yes, but Terry wants to practise his diving, so guess where he wants to go!

Girl: The lake?

Boy: No, he needs a diving board and the lake's no good for that.

Girl: Well, he can go to the sports centre with Sam.

Boy: The sports centre doesn't have a pool, and Sam's hurt his arm, so he can't play tennis. He said he wants to go to that exhibition of Japanese art instead.

Girl: Oh.

Now listen again.
That is the end of Part 5. You now have six minutes to write your answers on the answer sheet.
That is the end of the test.

TEST 8   SPEAKING

Part 1

Track 55

Examiner: Good afternoon.
Can I have your mark sheets, please? I'm Keira Benn. And this is Noel Connor.
What's your name, Candidate A?

Candidate A: My name's Apinya Saengsawang.

Examiner: And what's your name, Candidate B?

[PAUSE FOR YOU TO ANSWER]

Examiner: Candidate B, how old are you?

[PAUSE FOR YOU TO ANSWER]

Examiner: Where are you from, Candidate B?

[PAUSE FOR YOU TO ANSWER]

Examiner: Thank you.
Candidate A, how old are you?

Candidate A: I'm thirteen.

Examiner: Where are you from?

Candidate A: I'm from Thailand.

Examiner: Thank you.
Now, let's talk about festivals.
Candidate A, what is an important festival where you come from?

Candidate A: Songkran Festival is important in Thailand. It's also called the water festival and it's the start of the new year in Thailand.

Examiner: What do you do at Songkran?

Candidate A: We clean our houses before the festival and during the festival people throw water at each other.

Examiner: Candidate B, what is an important festival in your country?

[PAUSE FOR YOU TO ANSWER]

Examiner: What do you do during this festival, Candidate B?

[PAUSE FOR YOU TO ANSWER]

Examiner: Now, Candidate A, please tell me what you like best about your favourite festival.

Candidate A: Well, the water festival is my favourite. The best thing about it is playing with the water. You get very wet and have a lot of fun Everywhere you go, people throw water, so you don't wear your best clothes! There's delicious food to eat as well.

Examiner: Now, let's talk about going to the cinema.
Candidate B, do you often go to the cinema?

[PAUSE FOR YOU TO ANSWER]

Examiner: What kind of films do you watch, Candidate B?

[PAUSE FOR YOU TO ANSWER]

Examiner: Candidate A, do you often go to the cinema?

Candidate A: No, I don't.

Examiner: Why not?

Candidate A: My friends and I prefer to watch a film at home because the cinema is expensive. If you watch a film at home, you can talk to your friends about it at the same time.

Examiner: Now, Candidate B, can you tell me about the last time you went to the cinema?

[PAUSE FOR YOU TO ANSWER]

Examiner: Thank you.

Part 2

Track 56

Examiner: Now, in this part of the test you are going to talk together.
Here are some pictures that show different pets.
Do you like these different pets? Say why or why not. I'll say that again.
Do you like these different pets? Say why or why not.
All right? Now, talk together.

Candidate A: I think this picture shows a rabbit, and in my opinion, it's a good pet for a young child. Do you think a rabbit is a good pet?

[PAUSE FOR YOU TO ANSWER]

Candidate A: Mice might be good if you don't have a lot of space at home because they're small, but I don't think they're very interesting pets. You can watch them go around in their wheel, but they don't do much – and some people don't like mice!

[PAUSE FOR YOU TO ANSWER]

Candidate A: What about a dog?

[PAUSE FOR YOU TO ANSWER]

Candidate A: Yes, that's right, and you can play with it. You can throw a ball and it will bring it back to you.

[PAUSE FOR YOU TO ANSWER]

Candidate A: Yes, I would, if it's a friendly cat. Some cats aren't very friendly.

[PAUSE FOR YOU TO ANSWER]

Candidate A: Yes, I agree with you. People keep chickens for their eggs, but I don't think they're really pets.

[PAUSE FOR YOU TO ANSWER]

Candidate A: Yes, but I don't think I want to play with a chicken.

Examiner: Candidate A, you said a rabbit is a good pet for a young child. Why?

Candidate A: I think it's easy to look after a rabbit. You just have to give it some food and clean water and clean its home.

Examiner: Candidate B, you didn't say what you thought about having a mouse as a pet. Can you tell us now?

[PAUSE FOR YOU TO ANSWER]

Examiner: So, Candidate A, which of these pets do you like the best?

Candidate A: I think a dog is the best pet because you can have the most fun with it.

Examiner: And you, Candidate B, which of these pets do you like the best?

[PAUSE FOR YOU TO ANSWER]

Examiner: Thank you. Can I have the booklet, please?
Now, Candidate B, can you compare having a rabbit with having chickens?

[PAUSE FOR YOU TO ANSWER]

Examiner: And what about you, Candidate A? Can you compare having a cat with having a mouse?

Candidate A: They're very different pets. A cat doesn't always stay at home, so it'll go outside on its own. But a mouse has to stay in its cage all the time. You can take it out and play with it, but it might run away and you might lose it. You can also play with a cat, especially when it's young. The best thing about a cat is that it will sit on you and make you feel comfortable. You can't do that with a mouse. If you take it out of the cage, you have to watch it all the time.

Examiner: Candidate A, which of these pets do you think is the worst?

Candidate A: I think the chickens are the worst. You can't really do anything with them.

Examiner: Which of these pets do you think is the worst, Candidate B?

[PAUSE FOR YOU TO ANSWER]

Examiner: Thank you. That is the end of the test.

193

Sample answer sheets

58693

Cambridge Assessment
English

Candidate Name		Candidate Number	
Centre Name		Centre Number	
Examination Title		Examination Details	
Candidate Signature		Assessment Date	

Supervisor: If the candidate is ABSENT or has WITHDRAWN shade here ○

Key for Schools Reading and Writing Candidate Answer Sheet

Instructions

Use a PENCIL (B or HB).
Rub out any answer you want to change with an eraser.

For Parts 1, 2, 3 and 4:
Mark ONE letter for each answer.
For example: If you think A is the right answer to the question, mark your answer sheet like this:

0 A■ B○ C○

For Part 5:
Write your answers clearly in the spaces next to the numbers (25 to 30) like this:

0 ENGLISH

Write your answers in CAPITAL LETTERS.

Part 1	A B C
1	○ ○ ○
2	○ ○ ○
3	○ ○ ○
4	○ ○ ○
5	○ ○ ○
6	○ ○ ○

Part 2	A B C
7	○ ○ ○
8	○ ○ ○
9	○ ○ ○
10	○ ○ ○
11	○ ○ ○
12	○ ○ ○
13	○ ○ ○

Part 3	A B C
14	○ ○ ○
15	○ ○ ○
16	○ ○ ○
17	○ ○ ○
18	○ ○ ○

Part 4	A B C
19	○ ○ ○
20	○ ○ ○
21	○ ○ ○
22	○ ○ ○
23	○ ○ ○
24	○ ○ ○

Part 5		Do not write below here			Do not write below here
25		25 1 0 ○ ○	28		28 1 0 ○ ○
26		26 1 0 ○ ○	29		29 1 0 ○ ○
27		27 1 0 ○ ○	30		30 1 0 ○ ○

Put your answers to Writing Parts 6 and 7 on the separate Answer Sheet

58693

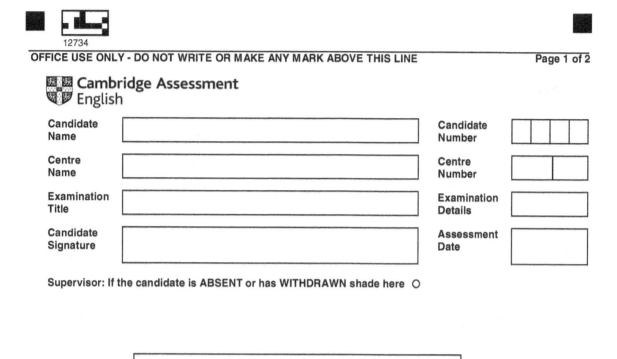

Cambridge Assessment
English

Candidate Name		Candidate Number	
Centre Name		Centre Number	
Examination Title		Examination Details	
Candidate Signature		Assessment Date	

Supervisor: If the candidate is ABSENT or has WITHDRAWN shade here ○

Key for Schools Writing

Candidate Answer Sheet for Parts 6 and 7

INSTRUCTIONS TO CANDIDATES

Make sure that your name and candidate number are on this sheet.

Write your answers to Writing Parts 6 and 7 on the other side of this sheet.

Use a pencil.

You **must** write within the grey lines.

Do **not** write on the bar codes.

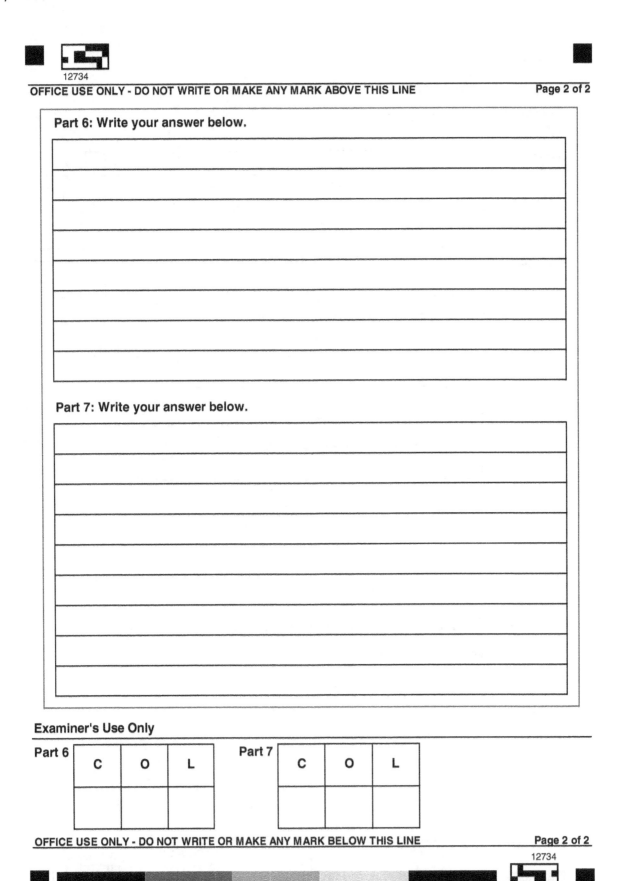

Part 6: Write your answer below.

Part 7: Write your answer below.

Examiner's Use Only

Part 6	C	O	L

Part 7	C	O	L

OFFICE USE ONLY - DO NOT WRITE OR MAKE ANY MARK BELOW THIS LINE   Page 2 of 2

12734

47288

 Cambridge Assessment
English

Candidate Name		Candidate Number	
Centre Name		Centre Number	
Examination Title		Examination Details	
Candidate Signature		Assessment Date	

Supervisor: If the candidate is ABSENT or has WITHDRAWN shade here ○

Key for Schools Listening Candidate Answer Sheet

Instructions
Use a PENCIL (B or HB).
Rub out any answer you want to change with an eraser.

For Parts 1, 3, 4 and 5:
Mark ONE letter for each answer.
For example: If you think A is the right answer to the question, mark your answer sheet like this:

0 A● B○ C○

For Part 2:
Write your answers clearly in the spaces next to the numbers (6 to 10) like this:

0 ENGLISH

Write your answers in CAPITAL LETTERS.

Part 1

	A	B	C
1	○	○	○
2	○	○	○
3	○	○	○
4	○	○	○
5	○	○	○

Part 2

		Do not write below here
6		6 1 0 ○ ○
7		7 1 0 ○ ○
8		8 1 0 ○ ○
9		9 1 0 ○ ○
10		10 1 0 ○ ○

Part 3

	A	B	C
11	○	○	○
12	○	○	○
13	○	○	○
14	○	○	○
15	○	○	○

Part 4

	A	B	C
16	○	○	○
17	○	○	○
18	○	○	○
19	○	○	○
20	○	○	○

Part 5

	A	B	C	D	E	F	G	H
21	○	○	○	○	○	○	○	○
22	○	○	○	○	○	○	○	○
23	○	○	○	○	○	○	○	○
24	○	○	○	○	○	○	○	○
25	○	○	○	○	○	○	○	○

47288

Answer key for Reading and Listening

This is the Answer key for the Reading and Listening parts of Tests 1-8.

TEST 1

Reading

Part 1
1 B
2 C
3 C
4 A
5 B
6 A

Part 2
7 C
8 B
9 C
10 A
11 A
12 B
13 C

Part 3
14 B
15 A
16 B
17 C
18 B

Part 4
19 C
20 B
21 A
22 A
23 B
24 C

Part 5
25 Do
26 would
27 on
28 the
29 as
30 me

Listening

Part 1
1 C
2 B
3 B
4 B
5 A

Part 2
6 Macilroy
7 café / cafe
8 12 / twelve
9 500
10 16th April / 16 April

Part 3
11 C
12 C
13 B
14 A
15 C

Part 4
16 A
17 A
18 B
19 C
20 A

Part 5
21 D
22 G
23 C
24 H
25 F

TEST 2

Reading

Part 1
1 A
2 C
3 C
4 B
5 A
6 B

Part 2
7 C
8 B
9 B
10 A
11 A
12 B
13 C

Part 3
14 B
15 A
16 B
17 A
18 C

Part 4
19 B
20 C
21 A
22 B
23 C
24 A

Part 5
25 at
26 how
27 are
28 was
29 Do
30 what

Listening

Part 1
1 B
2 B
3 A
4 B
5 C

Part 2
6 1 / one
7 fruit
8 farmers
9 10 / ten
10 14 / fourteen

Part 3
11 C
12 B
13 C
14 A
15 B

Part 4
16 C
17 A
18 B
19 A
20 A

Part 5
21 G
22 B
23 F
24 A
25 D

TEST 3

Reading

Part 1
1 C
2 B
3 A
4 B
5 C
6 C

Part 2
7 B
8 C
9 A
10 B
11 A
12 B
13 C

Part 3
14 C
15 C
16 C
17 A
18 B

Part 4
19 A
20 B
21 C
22 A
23 C
24 B

Part 5
25 one
26 Does
27 there
28 much
29 for / on
30 them

Listening

Part 1
1 C
2 B
3 B
4 C
5 A

Part 2
6 Wednesday
7 4.15
8 15
9 Schneider
10 £8

Part 3
11 B
12 A
13 B
14 C
15 C

Part 4
16 B
17 A
18 A
19 C
20 C

Part 5
21 E
22 A
23 C
24 H
25 F

TEST 4

Reading

Part 1
1 C
2 B
3 B
4 A
5 B
6 A

Part 2
7 C
8 C
9 B
10 C
11 A
12 A
13 B

Part 3
14 C
15 A
16 B
17 B
18 C

Part 4
19 A
20 C
21 A
22 B
23 A
24 C

Part 5
25 since
26 Has
27 have
28 like
29 the
30 it

Listening

Part 1
1 B
2 B
3 C
4 B
5 A

Part 2
6 8.15 (a.m.) / quarter past eight
7 lunchtime(s)
8 Howell
9 top
10 parents

Part 3
11 C
12 B
13 A
14 B
15 A

Part 4
16 A
17 A
18 C
19 A
20 B

Part 5
21 D
22 H
23 C
24 F
25 A

TEST 5

Reading

Part 1
1 B
2 A
3 A
4 B
5 B
6 C

Part 2
7 B
8 A
9 B
10 C
11 B
12 C
13 A

Part 3
14 B
15 B
16 A
17 B
18 C

Part 4
19 C
20 A
21 B
22 B
23 C
24 A

Part 5
25 on
26 there
27 they
28 to
29 be
30 me

Listening

Part 1
1 C
2 A
3 A
4 C
5 C

Part 2
6 gym
7 8.45 / quarter to nine
8 Challis
9 walking
10 750

Part 3
11 B
12 C
13 B
14 A
15 B

Part 4
16 A
17 B
18 A
19 C
20 C

Part 5
21 B
22 H
23 E
24 D
25 A

TEST 6

Reading

Part 1
1 A
2 C
3 B
4 C
5 C
6 B

Part 2
7 C
8 B
9 A
10 B
11 A
12 C
13 B

Part 3
14 C
15 A
16 C
17 A
18 B

Part 4
19 C
20 B
21 A
22 C
23 B
24 A

Part 5
25 some
26 Is
27 who
28 but
29 to
30 with

Listening

Part 1
1 A
2 B
3 B
4 C
5 A

Part 2
6 Kearnes
7 theatre
8 1,300
9 £5
10 14 March / 14th March

Part 3
11 C
12 B
13 C
14 A
15 A

Part 4
16 A
17 C
18 A
19 C
20 B

Part 5
21 C
22 D
23 H
24 F
25 E

TEST 7

Reading

Part 1
1 B
2 C
3 A
4 C
5 A
6 B

Part 2
7 B
8 A
9 B
10 B
11 C
12 A
13 C

Part 3
14 B
15 A
16 C
17 A
18 C

Part 4
19 C
20 B
21 B
22 A
23 A
24 C

Part 5
25 my
26 It
27 one
28 about
29 is
30 to

Listening

Part 1
1 C
2 C
3 A
4 C
5 B

Part 2
6 169
7 trains
8 2011
9 lake
10 glass

Part 3
11 C
12 B
13 B
14 A
15 A

Part 4
16 C
17 B
18 A
19 C
20 C

Part 5
21 A
22 G
23 B
24 H
25 C

TEST 8

Reading

Part 1
1 A
2 B
3 C
4 A
5 A
6 B

Part 2
7 A
8 C
9 A
10 B
11 C
12 B
13 B

Part 3
14 B
15 C
16 A
17 A
18 C

Part 4
19 C
20 B
21 C
22 A
23 B
24 A

Part 5
25 for
26 and
27 do
28 but
29 be
30 If

Listening

Part 1
1 B
2 C
3 C
4 A
5 C

Part 2
6 34
7 3 / three
8 999
9 medicine
10 unhappy

Part 3
11 A
12 B
13 A
14 C
15 A

Part 4
16 B
17 C
18 B
19 B
20 A

Part 5
21 H
22 D
23 A
24 C
25 B

Model answers for Writing

These are the model answers for the Writing parts of Tests 1–8.

Test 1

Writing Part 6

Question 31

> Hi Ellie,
> I'm really sorry, but I can't go shopping tomorrow. I'm sick! I feel terrible and I have to stay in bed.
> Would you like to go shopping next Saturday instead?

Writing Part 7

Question 32

One night Archie couldn't sleep because he had toothache. He was very unhappy. The next day, he went to the dentist. The dentist fixed his tooth and he felt much better. That night, when he went to bed, he slept very well.

Test 2

Writing Part 6

Question 31

> Hi Jay,
> Thank you so much for inviting me to lunch. I'd love to come. Can you tell me how to get to your house? I'll bring a basket of strawberries from our garden. We've got lots and we can have them with cream.

Writing Part 7

Question 32

One day Sarah saw some children riding their bikes in the park. She wanted to join them, but she couldn't ride a bike and she felt sad. The next day, her father helped her learn to ride. Sarah was very happy because she could play with the other children and ride her bike with them.

Test 3

Writing Part 6

Question 31

> Hi Tanya,
> Can you do me a favour? My bike is broken. I know you're good at repairing things, so can you help me fix it? If you can, when can you do it? And is there anything I can do for you?

Writing Part 7

Question 32

One day John went for a ride on his bike. His mother told him to wear a jacket, but he didn't listen to her. Then the weather changed. It started to rain and it was very windy. John got cold and wet. When he came back home, he felt ill and he went to bed. His mother looked after him.

Test 4

Writing Part 6

Question 31

> Hi Alex,
> I have a problem. I forgot my lunch money today and I can't buy anything to eat. Could I borrow some money from you? I'll give it back to you tomorrow.

Writing Part 7

Question 32

One day, Anna saw some girls eating ice cream. She wanted to have some ice cream too, but she didn't have any money. Then she washed her dad's car and he gave her some money. Anna went to the shop and bought an ice cream. She enjoyed it very much.

Test 5

Writing Part 6

Question 31

> Hi Natalie,
> Would you like to come to the park for a party on Saturday afternoon? We're meeting at City Park at two o'clock. Carla is bringing a barbecue. We're going to bring our own food to cook there, so bring something to cook too.

Writing Part 7

Question 32

Three months ago, Eric was in a running race at school. He wasn't very fit, so he couldn't run fast and he had to stop. Then Eric decided to go to the gym to get fit. He exercised very hard. The next time Eric ran in a race at school, he won it.

Test 6

Writing Part 6

Question 31

> Hi Marlon,
> Would it be possible to get a lift with you to school tomorrow? I've got lots of heavy books to carry. If your mum says it's all right, I can walk to the post office and you can pick me up there at eight o'clock.

Writing Part 7

Question 32

It was Davina's birthday and she invited her friends to a party. Her mum made her a birthday cake and put lots of food and drink on the table. Davina ate a lot of birthday cake and she drank a lot too so she felt sick.

Test 7

Writing Part 6

Question 31

Hi Bailey,
Could you take my book back to the library for me, please? I have to go and see my grandmother this afternoon, so I can't go. I can take your books back for you next time.

Writing Part 7

Question 32

Jamie was playing football one day. His football boots were very old and when he kicked the ball, one of his boots broke. He went shopping for some new football boots. When he played football again, he played very well.

Test 8

Writing Part 6

Question 31

Hi Ben,
I'm sorry I can't go to the cinema with you on Saturday. I've already planned to go out for a meal with my family. Would you like to go to the cinema next Saturday evening instead?

Writing Part 7

Question 32

The Smith family decided to go fishing one day. They took some food with them and went to the lake. Anna and Mark caught some fish and their parents sat and watched them. When they went home, they had the fish for dinner.

Model answers for Speaking

The model answers for the Speaking parts of Tests 1–8 are highlighted in grey here. You can listen to these model answers online at: www.collins.co.uk/eltresources

Test 1

Speaking Part 1

06a

Examiner:	Good morning.
	Can I have your mark sheets, please?
	I'm Frank Green. And this is Julia Turner.
	What's your name, Candidate A?
Candidate A:	My name's Afonso Silva.
Examiner:	And what's your name, Candidate B?
Candidate B:	My name's Sofia Santos.
Examiner:	Candidate B, how old are you?
Candidate B:	I'm thirteen.
Examiner:	Where do you live, Candidate B?
Candidate B:	I live in Alfama, near the castle.
Examiner:	Thank you.
	Candidate A, how old are you?
Candidate A:	I'm twelve.
Examiner:	Where do you live?
Candidate A:	I live in Belem.
Examiner:	Thank you.
	Now, let's talk about the area where you live.
	Candidate A, do you like the area where you live?
Candidate A:	Yes, I do. We have nice neighbours. The area is quiet and it's safe. I think it's a good place to live.
Examiner:	How long have you lived there?
Candidate A:	I've lived there all my life, so I know it very well. A lot of friends also live nearby.
Examiner:	Candidate B, what do you like about the area where you live?
Candidate B:	It's very pretty because it's the old part of town and it feels like a special place.
Examiner:	Is there anything you don't like about your area, Candidate B?
Candidate B:	Sometimes there are a lot of tourists. We live near the castle and tourists come to visit it. They can be noisy and they take up places in the restaurants and the cafés.
Examiner:	Now, Candidate A, please tell me about a place you would like to live if you could live anywhere.
Candidate A:	My grandparents have a house in the countryside. It's also very near the sea, so you can go to the beach and swim or you can play in the fields. I'd love to live in that area if I could.
Examiner:	Now, let's talk about sleeping. Candidate B, what time do you go to sleep at night?
Candidate B:	I usually go to sleep at about eleven o'clock at night, but sometimes it's later than that, and other times it's a bit earlier.
Examiner:	Do you sleep well, Candidate B?
Candidate B:	Not very well. I share my room with my sister and she sometimes wakes me up.
Examiner:	Candidate A, do you like sleeping?
Candidate A:	Yes, I do. When I go to bed, I read for a little while and then feel sleepy and I'm ready to go to sleep.
Examiner:	How much sleep do you need?
Candidate A:	I think I need about eight or nine hours. If I sleep from ten or eleven o'clock at night to seven or eight o'clock in the morning, then I feel good.

Examiner: Now Candidate B, please tell me if you think teenagers get enough sleep.

Candidate B: I think a lot of teenagers don't get enough sleep because there are lots of other things to do. For example, many people my age stay up late on their mobile phone or laptop, talking to friends and following social media. I think it's a big problem for young people.

Examiner: Thank you.

Speaking Part 2

07a

Examiner: Now, in this part of the test you are going to talk together.
Here are some pictures that show different ways of getting to school.
Do you like these different ways of getting to school? Say why or why not. I'll say that again. Do you like these different ways of getting to school? Say why or why not. All right? Now, talk together.

Candidate A: I think walking is a good way to get to school because it keeps you fit. Do you agree?

Candidate B: Yes, I think you're right. If you live close to the school, I think it's the best way to get there. It's cheap, it's good exercise and you won't be late.

Candidate A: What do you think about cycling to school?

Candidate B: I think cycling is also a good way to get to school every day. It also keeps you fit, like walking, but it's faster than walking. But it's not so good when it's raining.

Candidate A: No, it isn't. You'd get very wet and you don't want to be wet all day at school. And you have to look after your bike, keep it in good condition so it works well.

Candidate B: Yes, that's right. You have to lock it up so nobody steals it. And you might get a flat tyre sometimes, so you have to be able to repair it.

Candidate A: What do you think about getting a lift from your parents?

Candidate B: I think it's the easiest way to get there. You go from your front door all the way to school and you don't have to do anything yourself. What do you think about getting the bus to school?

Candidate A: Well, a lot of children go to school by bus and there's often a bus stop outside a school. Finally, what about going to school by taxi?

Candidate B: It's an easy way to get there, but it must be very expensive, especially if you live a long way away!

Candidate A: Yes, I agree with you.

Examiner: Candidate A, do you like going to school by bus?

Candidate A: No, I don't.

Examiner: Why not?

Candidate A: I like to have a quiet time in the morning, but buses are usually very crowded and noisy. Also, if there are a lot of people on the bus, it isn't a comfortable way to travel.

Examiner: Candidate B, do you like walking to school?

Candidate B: Yes, I like it very much. I walked to school when I was at primary school and it was fun. After school, you walk back home with your friends and play games with them as you walk along.

Examiner: So, Candidate A, which of these ways of getting to school do you like the best?

Candidate A: I think walking is the best way – unless the weather is bad.

Examiner: And you, Candidate B, which of these ways of getting to school do you like the best?

Candidate B: I agree with Afonso. I think walking is the best way. It's the most fun way.

Examiner: Thank you. Can I have the booklet, please?
Now, Candidate B, can you compare walking to school to getting to school by bus?

Candidate B: In my opinion, they are very different. If you walk, you get exercise and fresh air. You can easily stop somewhere like a shop if you need to. But when you get on a bus, you have to stay on it until you get to school.

Examiner: And what about you, Candidate A? Can you compare walking to school with getting a lift from your parents?

Candidate A:	Going to school by car is very comfortable, but it might be boring if you have to go home with them immediately after school. I like to see my friends after school, so I prefer to walk home with them.
Examiner:	Candidate A, which of these ways of getting to school do you think is the worst?
Candidate A:	I think cycling is the worst way.
Examiner:	Why?
Candidate A:	I don't like cycling because I get hot. I also think it's dangerous because of the traffic.
Examiner:	Which of these ways of getting to school do you think is the worst, Candidate B?
Candidate B:	In my opinion, the bus is the worst. It's uncomfortable and when there are a lot of people, you might have to stand up all the way. You also have to wait at bus stops and you might miss it if you're a little late.
Examiner:	Thank you. That is the end of the test.

Test 2

Speaking Part 1

🎧
13a

Examiner:	Good afternoon.
	Can I have your mark sheets, please?
	I'm Meg Gibsy. And this is Scott Stevens.
	What's your name, Candidate A?
Candidate A:	My name's Magdalena Nowak.
Examiner:	And what's your name, Candidate B?
Candidate B:	My name's Dmitri Turgenev.
Examiner:	Candidate B, how old are you?
Candidate B:	I'm fourteen.
Examiner:	Where are you from, Candidate B?
Candidate B:	I'm from Moscow, in Russia.
Examiner:	Thank you.
	Candidate A, how old are you?
Candidate A:	I'm thirteen.
Examiner:	Where are you from?
Candidate A:	I'm from Warsaw in Poland.
Examiner:	Thank you.
	Now, let's talk about presents.
	Candidate A, do you like to give or receive presents?
Candidate A:	I prefer to receive presents. It's exciting to get them.
Examiner:	Who gives you presents and when do they give them to you?
Candidate A:	My parents give me presents on my birthday and they also give me presents at Christmas.
Examiner:	Candidate B, do you like to give or receive presents?
Candidate B:	Of course, I like to receive presents, but it's also nice to give presents to other people because it makes them happy.
Examiner:	When was the last time you got a present, Candidate B?
Candidate B:	The last present I got was on my birthday.
Examiner:	Now, Candidate A, please tell me about a present that you got that you were really happy with.
Candidate A:	My parents gave me a mobile phone on my twelfth birthday and I was very happy to get it. It was my first phone. Before then, they said I was too young to have one.
Examiner:	Now, let's talk about your future.
	Candidate B, do you know what you would like to do after you have finished school?
Candidate B:	I'm not sure. If I do well at school, then I'd like to go to university.
Examiner:	Where would you like to go to university, Candidate B?
Candidate B:	I'd like to go to one of the top universities in my country.

Examiner:	Candidate A, do you know what you would like to do after you have finished school?
Candidate A:	Yes, I do. I want to go to university and study to be a doctor.
Examiner:	Why do you want to be a doctor?
Candidate A:	Both my parents are doctors and I think the job they do is very important. They help people when they're sick and I'd like to do that too.
Examiner:	Now, Candidate B, please tell me if you think young people should plan their future carefully.
Candidate B:	I don't think that young people should plan their future very carefully because a person might change their mind about what they want to do in the future. It's good to have an idea, but it's also good to change your mind about something if you need to.
Examiner:	Thank you.

Speaking Part 2

14a

Examiner:	Now, in this part of the test you are going to talk together. Here are some pictures that show different games. Do you like these different games? Say why or why not. I'll say that again. Do you like these different games? Say why or why not. All right? Now, talk together.
Candidate A:	I think badminton is a fun game and I really enjoy playing it. Do you like it?
Candidate B:	Yes, I like it too. You can play it in the garden and you can easily take your racket anywhere to play it.
Candidate A:	How do you feel about basketball?
Candidate B:	It's an exciting game because it's so fast, and the good thing about it is that you can practise it on your own.
Candidate A:	Yes, you're right. You can practise throwing the ball at the basket even when you're alone. With the other games, you need people to play with you.
Candidate B:	Yes. I have a basketball and I play on my own sometimes.
Candidate A:	What about tennis?
Candidate B:	I don't like it very much. I've only played it a few times and I'm not good at it. Perhaps I'd like it more if I were a good player. What do you think about football?
Candidate A:	I think it's a boring game. I played football with my brothers when I was younger. I was the goalkeeper, but I always let the ball go into the net.
Candidate B:	I enjoy football. It's a good game to play with a group of friends and everybody can join in.
Candidate A:	Yes, that's true. A lot of people can play together.
Examiner:	Candidate A, do you like playing table tennis?
Candidate A:	Yes, I do. It's one of my favourite games.
Examiner:	What do you like about it?
Candidate A:	It's easy to play. Even if you aren't very good, you can have a fun time.
Examiner:	Candidate B, do you like playing table tennis?
Candidate B:	No, I don't. You just hit a little ball, so I don't think it's very interesting.
Examiner:	So, Candidate A, which of these games do you like the best?
Candidate A:	I think badminton is the best game. It's easy to play and it doesn't matter if you aren't very good at it.
Examiner:	And you, Candidate B, which of these games do you like the best?
Candidate B:	I like football the best. I enjoy playing it and I love watching it too.
Examiner:	Thank you. Can I have the booklet, please? Now, Candidate B, can you compare basketball with football?
Candidate B:	Yes. Football is very popular. People all over the world play it and it's always on television. It's much more popular than basketball. Goals don't happen very often in football, but players score all the time in basketball. That makes it exciting.
Examiner:	And what about you, Candidate A? Can you compare badminton to tennis?
Candidate A:	I think they're very different games. Badminton is slower and easier to play than tennis. You can take your badminton racket anywhere, and you don't have to play with a net.

For example, you can even play badminton at the beach. Tennis is more serious and you need to play on a tennis court.

Examiner: Candidate A which of these games do you like the least?

Candidate A: I like football the least.

Examiner: Why?

Candidate A: Everybody gets too excited. Everybody shouts at everybody. I don't think it's a nice game.

Examiner: Which of these games do you like the least, Candidate B?

Candidate B: My least favourite game is tennis. I think it's a difficult game to play well. If you aren't good at it, you have to keep stopping and starting. It's difficult to hit the ball well and you have to keep going to pick up the balls.

Examiner: Thank you. That is the end of the test.

Test 3

Speaking Part 1

🎧
20a

Examiner: Good evening.
Can I have your mark sheets, please?
I'm Kyle Hayes. And this is Tina Day.
What's your name, Candidate A?

Candidate A: My name's Juan Garcia.

Examiner: And what's your name, Candidate B?

Candidate B: My name's Elena Gonzalez.

Examiner: Candidate B, how old are you?

Candidate B: I'm thirteen.

Examiner: Where do you live, Candidate B?

Candidate B I live in Buenos Aires.

Examiner: Thank you.
Candidate A, how old are you?

Candidate A: I'm thirteen too.

Examiner: Where do you live?

Candidate A: I live in Buenos Aires as well, but I'm from Cordoba.

Examiner: Thank you.
Now, let's talk about your homes.
Candidate A, can you tell me about your home?

Candidate A: Yes, I live in an apartment in a big block. You have to take a lift to go up to it. It's on the sixth floor.

Examiner: What is it like inside?

Candidate A: It isn't very big, but it's nice. There are two bedrooms, one for my parents and one for me and my brother.

Examiner: Candidate B, can you tell me about your home?

Candidate B: I live in a house with a small garden. It's very nice to have a garden, but my house is a long way from the city centre.

Examiner: What is it like inside, Candidate B?

Candidate B: There's a lot of space. We have a big living room and the dining room and the kitchen are together in the same room. Upstairs there are three bedrooms.

Examiner: Now, Candidate A, is there anything that you don't like about your home?

Candidate A: I don't like being in an apartment block. It means I have to go down in the lift every time I want to go outside or play football. I'd like to have a garden.

Examiner: Now, let's talk about reading.
Candidate B, what kind of things do you read?

Candidate B: I read a lot. I've read all the Ruby Redfort books. I like books like that, with an exciting story.

Examiner: How often do you read, Candidate B?

Candidate B: I read every day. I sometimes read on the bus and I always read at night.
Examiner: Candidate A, what kind of things do you read?
Candidate A: I read when I study, but I don't often read outside school.
Examiner: Why don't you like reading?
Candidate A: I prefer to watch things on television or on the internet. I don't think books are as interesting as watching and listening. Reading feels like work to me.
Examiner: Now, Candidate B, please tell me about something you have read recently.
Candidate B: I've just finished reading a book called *The River*. It's a book we're studying at school and it's about a girl who lives near a river. She swims in it every day, but one day the water stops and there isn't a river anymore. Then she and her friends go on an adventure and find out why the river has disappeared.
Examiner: Thank you.

Speaking Part 2

21a

Examiner: Now, in this part of the test you are going to talk together.
Here are some pictures that show different places to eat.
Do you like these different places to eat? Say why or why not. I'll say that again.
Do you like these different places to eat? Say why or why not.
All right? Now, talk together.
Candidate A: In my opinion, a fast food restaurant is a good place to eat. What do you think?
Candidate B: Well, I don't agree. I don't like fast food very much and I'd prefer to eat in a nice restaurant.
Candidate A: Do you mean like this restaurant on a boat?
Candidate B: No, I mean a normal restaurant, inside, like this one. The food is much better there. Do you like having picnics?
Candidate A: Yes, very much. It's fun to have a picnic. You can enjoy playing football outside, and then you can stop and eat for a bit, and then you can play some more.
Candidate B: Yes, I like picnics too. If the weather's good, my parents often take me and my sister somewhere nice for a picnic.
Candidate A: Where do you go?
Candidate B: We sometimes go to the park because it's close to our house. And sometimes we go to the beach for the day and take a picnic. But it's quite a long way to the beach, so we don't do that very often. What about you?
Candidate A: Yes, we also take a picnic to the beach sometimes. That's my favourite place. What's your opinion about eating at home?
Candidate B: That's what we usually do. My mother and father are good cooks and I like eating the food they make.
Candidate A: Yes, I like eating at home too, but it's nice to go somewhere else to eat sometimes.
Examiner: Candidate A, would you like to eat at a restaurant on a boat?
Candidate A: Yes, I think so.
Examiner: Why?
Candidate A: It looks interesting. You can look around and enjoy the view while you eat.
Examiner: Candidate B, would you like to eat at a restaurant on a boat?
Candidate B: I don't know. You need to have good weather. On this boat the table is outside, so if it rains, your food and things will get wet.
Examiner: So, Candidate A, which of these places to eat do you like the best?
Candidate A: I think the fast food restaurant is the best place to eat.
Examiner: And you, Candidate B, which of these places to eat do you like the best?
Candidate B: I think a nice restaurant, indoors, is the best place to eat.
Examiner: Thank you. Can I have the booklet, please?
Examiner: Now, Candidate B, can you compare eating on a boat with eating inside at a nice restaurant?

Candidate B:	Yes. I think it's safer to eat in a normal restaurant inside. The restaurant here looks expensive, so the food will be good. You can talk and let the waiters serve you. On the boat, it might be windy, and the boat might move around a lot if the water isn't calm.
Examiner:	And what about you, Candidate A? Can you compare eating at a fast food restaurant to eating at a more expensive indoor restaurant?
Candidate A:	For me, eating at a fast food restaurant is better. I like food like burgers and French fries more than the kind of food they have in expensive restaurants. And you can wear jeans and a T-shirt, so it's more comfortable.
Examiner:	Candidate A, which of these places to eat is your least favourite?
Candidate A:	I think the expensive indoor restaurant is the worst.
Examiner:	Why?
Candidate A:	Well, as I said, it isn't very comfortable and I don't really like the food. Also, it takes a long time to eat a meal in an expensive restaurant and it's boring. I don't like sitting still and talking for a long time.
Examiner:	Which of these places to eat do you think is the worst, Candidate B?
Candidate B:	In my opinion, the fast food restaurant is the worst place to eat. I don't agree with Candidate A. I don't think the food is very nice and sometimes the tables are dirty. I only go there if I have to.
Examiner:	Thank you. That is the end of the test.

Test 4

Speaking Part 1

27a

Examiner:	Good morning. Can I have your mark sheets, please? I'm Lydia Miles. And this is Richard Molina. What's your name, Candidate A?
Candidate A:	My name's Yanjun Hu.
Examiner:	And what's your name, Candidate B?
Candidate B:	My name's Paulo Martins.
Examiner:	Candidate B, how old are you?
Candidate B:	I'm thirteen.
Examiner:	Where do you come from, Candidate B?
Candidate B:	I come from São Paulo in Brazil.
Examiner:	Thank you. Candidate A, how old are you?
Candidate A:	I'm twelve.
Examiner:	Where are you from?
Candidate A:	I'm from Shanghai, in China.
Examiner:	Thank you.
Examiner:	Now, let's talk about birthdays. Candidate A, do you usually do anything special on your birthday?
Candidate A:	Yes, I do. We usually go to a restaurant on my birthday to have a big meal.
Examiner:	Who goes to the restaurant?
Candidate A:	My parents and my grandparents come and I also invite some of my friends.
Examiner:	Candidate B, do you usually do anything special on your birthday?
Candidate B:	Yes, I do. A birthday is a very special day for young people in my country and I always have a party with a big cake.
Examiner:	Do you get presents on your birthday, Candidate B?
Candidate B:	Yes, from my parents. Friends come to the party, but they don't bring me presents. Only members of the family give me something.
Examiner:	Now, Candidate A, please tell me about your last birthday.

Candidate A:	I was at home in Shanghai and it was a school day, so I went to school. The class sang 'Happy Birthday' to me. Then after school, we went to my favourite restaurant to celebrate. We stayed at the restaurant for a long time. It was a great day.
Examiner:	Now, let's talk about musical instruments. Candidate B, do you play any musical instruments?
Candidate B:	I can play the guitar a little. I'm not very good at it, but I enjoy playing.
Examiner:	What kind of things do you play, Candidate B?
Candidate B:	I can play some pop songs – songs that everybody knows.
Examiner:	Candidate A, do you play a musical instrument?
Candidate A:	Yes, I play the piano. My parents wanted me to learn and I started when I was in primary school.
Examiner:	What kind of music do you play?
Candidate A:	I play classical music because that's what my parents wanted me to do, but actually, I haven't played very much over the last year.
Examiner:	Now, Candidate B, what musical instrument would you like to play well?
Candidate B:	I'd love to play the electric guitar well. It would be great to make a band with my friends and play songs. I think that would be fun.
Examiner:	Thank you.

Speaking Part 2

28a

Examiner:	Now, in this part of the test you are going to talk together. Here are some pictures that show different school clubs. Do you like these different school clubs? Say why or why not. I'll say that again. Do you like these different school clubs? Say why or why not. All right? Now, talk together.
Candidate A:	I think the chess club is a good one to join. Do you agree?
Candidate B:	I'm not sure. I can play chess, but I don't play it very well. It's a difficult game. Do you play it?
Candidate A:	Yes, I do. It's a popular club in my school in China, but I didn't join it. What do you think about the computer club?
Candidate B:	Actually, I wouldn't be interested in it. I think it's for people who want to learn how a computer works, but I'm not very interested in what happens inside a computer. What about you? Are you interested in the computer club?
Candidate A:	No, I don't think so. I think the same as you. What about cooking?
Candidate B:	Yes, that's a great club. It would be good if I could learn how to make some good dishes. I can't cook, but I want to learn. Would you like to go to the cooking club?
Candidate A:	Yes, I think it's a good club to join. I can't cook anything either. Would you like to go to the dance club?
Candidate B:	Dancing isn't for me. I can dance at parties, but I don't want to do this sort of dancing. How about you?
Candidate A:	Yes, it's fun and I'd like to learn to dance well. I think going to a dance club is a good way to meet other people and you can keep fit.
Candidate B:	You can meet other people at all the clubs.
Candidate A:	Yes, of course! You are right about that.
Examiner:	Candidate A, would you like to join a singing club?
Candidate A:	No, I wouldn't.
Examiner:	Why not?
Candidate A:	I'm terrible at singing and I think people would laugh at me if I went there. I don't think they'd let me join!
Examiner:	Candidate B, would you like to join a singing club?
Candidate B:	No, I feel the same as Yanjun. I think if I went to a singing club and the people there heard me sing, they'd ask me not to come back!
Examiner:	So, Candidate A, which of these school clubs do you like the best?
Candidate A:	I think the dance club is the best. If you go with your friends, you can have a lot of fun.

Examiner:	And you, Candidate B, which of these school clubs do you like the best?
Candidate B:	I think the cooking club is the best. Then I can cook some delicious meals for my friends and my family.
Examiner:	Thank you. Can I have the booklet, please?
Examiner:	Now, Candidate B, can you compare the chess club with the computer club?
Candidate B:	In my opinion, they're similar. The same people might go to both clubs. They're for people who like thinking, who like to use their brains. If you're good at chess, I think you're also good with computers. Maybe these clubs are good for clever students.
Examiner:	And what about you, Candidate A? Can you compare the singing club and the dance club?
Candidate A:	I also think these clubs are similar. They're for people who like to be active. But I think singing is a group activity. If you sing in a group, people can't hear just you, but when you dance, everybody can see you dancing.
Examiner:	Candidate A, which of these school clubs do you think is the worst?
Candidate A:	I think the computer club is the worst.
Examiner:	Why?
Candidate A:	I'm not interested in computers. I only use them for school work. I'm not interested in learning about them.
Examiner:	Which of these clubs do you think is the worst, Candidate B?
Candidate B:	In my opinion, the chess club is the worst. Players just sit and think and look at the board for a long time. I think it's boring, so it's my least favourite school club.
Examiner:	Thank you. That is the end of the test.

Test 5

Speaking Part 1

🎧
34a

Examiner:	Good afternoon.
	Can I have your mark sheets, please?
	I'm Michael Bates. And this is Rose Shipton.
	What's your name, Candidate A?
Candidate A:	My name's Laszlo Nagy.
Examiner:	And what's your name, Candidate B?
Candidate B:	My name's Hanna Horvath.
Examiner:	Candidate B, how old are you?
Candidate B:	I'm twelve.
Examiner:	Where do you live, Candidate B?
Candidate B:	I live here in Budapest.
Examiner:	Thank you.
	Candidate A, how old are you?
Candidate A:	I'm twelve too.
Examiner:	Where do you live?
Candidate A:	I also live in Budapest.
Examiner:	Thank you.
Examiner:	Now, let's talk about travel.
	Candidate A, do you often travel to other countries?
Candidate A:	Yes, I do. My parents like to go to new places and during the school holidays, we often travel outside Hungary.
Examiner:	Where was the last place you went to outside Hungary?
Candidate A:	The last time we travelled outside Hungary, we went to Croatia and spent two weeks at the seaside there.
Examiner:	Candidate B, do you often travel to other countries?
Candidate B:	Not very often. I've been to France and Germany, but we usually have our holidays at Lake Balaton. We have a house there.

Model answers: Speaking

Examiner:	Can you tell me about the last time you travelled, Candidate B?
Candidate B:	It was a long time ago and I was just a little girl, so I can't remember very much. We went to Paris and I remember we went up the Eiffel Tower and had a good view of the city.
Examiner:	Now, Candidate A, please tell me about a place you would like to travel to.
Candidate A:	I'd love to travel to the USA and visit Los Angeles and California. I like watching American films and I'd like to see the places where they make the films.
Examiner:	Now, let's talk about brothers and sisters. Candidate B, do you have any brothers and sisters?
Candidate B:	I have a brother.
Examiner:	What's he like, Candidate B?
Candidate B:	He's still very young. He's only six and he makes a lot of noise when he plays and runs around the house.
Examiner:	Candidate A, do you have any brothers and sisters?
Candidate A:	Yes, I have a brother and a sister.
Examiner:	What are they like?
Candidate A:	They're very nice. They're older than me and they help me with my homework.
Examiner:	Now, Candidate B, what is the best thing about having a brother?
Candidate B:	I wouldn't like to be an only child, and I'm glad I have a brother because I can play with him. But sometimes I have to look after him and that's not always easy.
Examiner:	Thank you.

Speaking Part 2

🎧
35a

Examiner:	Now, in this part of the test you are going to talk together. Here are some pictures that show different presents for people who have just got married. Do you like these different presents for people who have just got married? Say why or why not. I'll say that again. Do you like these different presents for people who have just got married? Say why or why not. All right? Now, talk together.
Candidate A:	This first picture is a clock. It's a beautiful clock and I think it's also a useful present to give people who have just got married. What do you think?
Candidate B:	Yes, I agree that it's a good present. It's something you can keep for a long time, and it's useful as well because it tells you the time. What do you think of the table?
Candidate A:	It looks like a little table for the living room where you put things like magazines or glasses. I think it's called a coffee table. When people get married, they often need furniture, so it's another useful present.
Candidate B:	I'm not sure about the table. It's a bit old-fashioned. I think young people would like something more modern. The next picture is a mirror, I think. It's a nice big mirror. In my opinion, it's another good present and you could put it in the bedroom.
Candidate A:	Yes, you could, but you could have it in another part of the house where everybody can see it, for example in the living room or the hall.
Candidate B:	Yes, good idea. It would be good in the hall. Then people can look in it to see themselves before they go out.
Candidate A:	Then there are these glasses. What do you think of them?
Candidate B:	If they're expensive glasses for special events, then they're a good present. But if they're just for every day, I don't think they're a very good present.
Candidate A:	Yes, I think you're right. The last present is money.
Candidate B:	Yes. Everybody likes to have money!
Candidate A:	But if you give people money, they know exactly how much you're giving them!
Examiner:	Candidate A, would you like somebody to give you money if you got married?
Candidate A:	I think so, yes.
Examiner:	Why?

Candidate A:	If somebody gives you money, you can buy what you want. Sometimes when people get married, they might get two presents that are the same!
Examiner:	Candidate B, would you like somebody to give you money if you got married?
Candidate B:	No, I wouldn't. I'd like to get a real present from them. When you get a real present, it shows that somebody thought about what I'd like and it's more personal.
Examiner:	So, Candidate A, which of these wedding presents do you like the best?
Candidate A:	I think a mirror is the best because it's the most useful. Everybody can use a mirror.
Examiner:	And you, Candidate B, which of these wedding presents do you like the best?
Candidate B:	I think a clock is the best. If it's a good clock, you'll have it for many, many years.
Examiner:	Thank you. Can I have the booklet, please?
Examiner:	Now, Candidate B, can you compare the clock with the glasses?
Candidate B:	Well, in my view, a clock is a better present than the glasses. It's true that everybody needs glasses, but they break, so you won't have them forever. But you have a clock forever, and you can give it to your children when you get old.
Examiner:	And what about you, Candidate A? Can you compare the coffee table with the mirror?
Candidate A:	I think they're both good presents. You have to be careful with a mirror because it can break, and if you break one, you'll have bad luck! I don't think you can break a table easily. But you should be careful when you put something on it because you might make a mark on it.
Examiner:	Candidate A, which of these presents do you think is the worst?
Candidate A:	I think the glasses are the worst present.
Examiner:	Why?
Candidate A:	I don't think they're interesting.
Examiner:	Which of these wedding presents do you think is the worst, Candidate B?
Candidate B:	In my opinion, the money and the glasses are both the worst. I wouldn't want to get them as a present.
Examiner:	Thank you. That is the end of the test.

Test 6

Speaking Part 1

🎧
41a

Examiner:	Good evening.
	Can I have your mark sheets, please?
	I'm Theresa Wood. And this is David Stillwell.
	What's your name, Candidate A?
Candidate A:	My name's Margarita Lopez.
Examiner:	And what's your name, Candidate B?
Candidate B:	My name's Akito Nakamura.
Examiner:	Candidate B, how old are you?
Candidate B:	I'm twelve.
Examiner:	Where are you from, Candidate B?
Candidate B:	I'm from Japan.
Examiner:	Thank you.
	Candidate A, how old are you?
Candidate A:	I'm thirteen.
Examiner:	Where are you from?
Candidate A:	I'm from Mexico.
Examiner:	Thank you.
Examiner:	Now, let's talk about keeping fit.
	Candidate A, what do you do to keep fit?
Candidate A:	I play lots of sport. I play basketball and badminton.
Examiner:	Where do you play them?
Candidate A:	I play basketball at school and I play badminton at home with my sister.

Examiner:	Candidate B, what do you do to keep fit?
Candidate B:	I love playing basketball. I play it every day and I'm in the school team. I also play it at home and with my friends.
Examiner:	What do you like so much about that sport, Candidate B?
Candidate B:	It's a great game – it's exciting and it's fast, and there are lots of baskets in basketball. I watch NBA on television all the time.
Examiner:	Now, Candidate A, do you think it is important to keep fit?
Candidate A:	Yes, I do.
Examiner:	Why?
Candidate A:	I don't want to put on weight or be unhealthy. If you're fit, you feel good and you're happy. You do better in life and you enjoy more activities.
Examiner:	Now, let's talk about exams at school. Candidate B, how do you feel about school exams?
Candidate B:	I don't like doing exams at all.
Examiner:	Why not, Candidate B?
Candidate B:	It's important to do well, but they're very hard. My parents always want to know what marks I get and they get upset if I don't get good marks.
Examiner:	Candidate A, how do you feel about school exams?
Candidate A:	Exams are OK for me.
Examiner:	Aren't they hard?
Candidate A:	They aren't too hard and my parents don't worry too much about my marks. They help me, they want me to do well, but they don't get upset if I get a bad mark.
Examiner:	Now, Candidate B, can you tell me about an exam where you did very well or badly?
Candidate B:	Last year I had a maths exam and I did very badly. My parents were unhappy. I tried my best, but I'm not good at maths. I think it's my worst subject at school.
Examiner:	Thank you.

Speaking Part 2

🎧 42a

Examiner:	Now, in this part of the test you are going to talk together. Here are some pictures that show different family days out. Do you like these different family days out? Say why or why not. I'll say that again. Do you like these different family days out? Say why or why not. All right? Now, talk together.
Candidate A:	The first day out is a trip to the zoo. I think it's quite a good day out. Do you agree?
Candidate B:	Yes, I do. You can see lots of different animals, you can learn a lot, and you can have fun as well. Next, there's a museum. What do you think about going to a museum for a day out?
Candidate A:	It might be good if it's an interesting museum, but some museums are boring.
Candidate B:	I agree with you. I've been to some very good ones, but I've also been to some that I didn't like at all.
Candidate A:	The next one is a shopping centre. We often go to one with my family. In my opinion, it's a good way to spend the day. You can buy some new clothes and you can have something to eat there as well.
Candidate B:	Oh, this time I don't agree with you. I don't like going to a shopping centre all day with my family. I'd prefer to go to one with my friends.
Candidate A:	What about going to the park? I think that's a good day out, especially if the children are young.
Candidate B:	Yes, I agree with you. It's good for young children because they can do whatever they want there.
Candidate A:	And finally, the water park. I think the water park is great. It's a really good day out for the family.
Candidate B:	Yes, you're right. The water park looks like a lot of fun.
Examiner:	Candidate A, you said the water park is great. Why do you say that?

Candidate A:	There are different things you can do. You can go for a swim, you can lie in the sun, and, of course, there are slides. Some of them are really big and you can go down them really fast. It's exciting.
Examiner:	Candidate B, you said young children can do whatever they like in the park. What sort of things do children do in a park?
Candidate B:	They play football and they run around. If there's a small lake, they can sail boats on the water. And the whole family can have a picnic.
Examiner:	So, Candidate A, which of these family days out do you like the best?
Candidate A:	I think the water park is the best day out.
Examiner:	And you, Candidate B, which of these days out do you think is the best?
Candidate B:	I have the same opinion as Margarita. I think the water park is the best day out.
Examiner:	Thank you. Can I have the booklet, please?
Examiner:	Now, Candidate B, can you compare going to the zoo with going to the museum?
Candidate B:	Yes. I think the zoo is more interesting. In both places you look at things, but at the zoo, you see living animals and you can get close to them. In a museum, you see old things and often they're quite boring.
Examiner:	And what about you, Candidate A? Can you compare going to a shopping centre with going to the zoo?
Candidate A:	They're very different activities. If you go to a zoo, you see nature, but a shopping centre is nothing like nature. It's indoors and you don't get any fresh air. But if the weather is bad or if it's too hot outside, a shopping centre can be comfortable.
Examiner:	Candidate A, which of these days out do you think is the worst?
Candidate A:	I think the museum is the worst.
Examiner:	Why?
Candidate A:	Museums are usually full of old things and most of them are boring.
Examiner:	Which of these days out do you think is the worst, Candidate B?
Candidate B:	I have the same opinion. I think the museum is the worst day out. The others are more fun.
Examiner:	Thank you. That is the end of the test.

Test 7

Speaking Part 1

48a

Examiner:	Good morning.
	Can I have your mark sheets, please?
	I'm Owen Taylor. And this is Hilary Dunn.
	What's your name, Candidate A?
Candidate A:	My name's Filip Kohel.
Examiner:	And what's your name, Candidate B?
Candidate B:	My name's Miroslava Zidek.
Examiner:	Candidate B, how old are you?
Candidate B:	I'm twelve.
Examiner:	Where do you live, Candidate B?
Candidate B:	I live in Prague.
Examiner:	Thank you.
	Candidate A, how old are you?
Candidate A:	I'm thirteen.
Examiner:	Where do you live?
Candidate A:	I live in Prague, but I come from Brno.
Examiner:	Thank you.
	Now, let's talk about neighbours.
	Candidate A, what are your neighbours like?

Candidate A:	I live in a flat, so I have a lot of neighbours. I don't know them all, but the ones on our floor are very nice.
Examiner:	Can you tell me about the neighbours who live the closest to you?
Candidate A:	They're an old man and his wife. I know them well because sometimes they looked after me when I was small.
Examiner:	Candidate B, do you have neighbours?
Candidate B:	Yes, I do. I live in a house and we have neighbours on one side of our house, but there's no house on the other side, so we just have one set of neighbours.
Examiner:	What are they like, Candidate B?
Candidate B:	They're a family like us. The children are much older than me and my brother. We don't see them very much because they aren't often at home and we don't know them well.
Examiner:	Now, Candidate A, please tell me what you think makes a good neighbour.
Candidate A:	A good neighbour will help you if you have a problem, for example, if you need something. You can knock on their door, ask for what you need and they'll help you.
Examiner:	Now, let's talk about what sort of person you are. Candidate B, do you think you are a happy person?
Candidate B:	Sometimes.
Examiner:	What makes you happy, Candidate B?
Candidate B:	I'm happy when I don't have to go to school or do homework. I'm happy in the school holidays.
Examiner:	Candidate A, what sort of person are you? Are you quiet or do you talk a lot?
Candidate A:	I think I talk a lot.
Examiner:	Who do you talk with and what about?
Candidate A:	I talk with my friends all the time. My teachers in school sometimes get angry because I talk too much in class.
Examiner:	Now, Candidate B, can you tell me what you do if you have had a bad day and you want to feel better?
Candidate B:	I go to my best friend's house. Her name is Michaela. We always talk about things together. If I have a problem, she helps me with it, or we just laugh about things and maybe watch a film. Then I feel much happier.
Examiner:	Thank you.

Speaking Part 2

49a

Examiner:	Now, in this part of the test you are going to talk together. Here are some pictures that show different jobs. Do you like these different jobs? Say why or why not. I'll say that again. Do you like these different jobs? Say why or why not. All right? Now, talk together.
Candidate A:	The first picture is somebody working in a library. Do you think that's a good job?
Candidate B:	Yes, it's a very nice job. It's quiet and I think it's quite an easy one. I'd like to be a librarian. What do you think of it?
Candidate A:	I don't think I'd like to work in a library, but it would be great for somebody who loves books and reading. What about being a doctor?
Candidate B:	Yes, I think being a doctor is a really good job. It's difficult and you have to study hard if you want to become a doctor.
Candidate A:	Yes, I agree with you. My parents would like me to be a doctor.
Candidate B:	The next picture is of a shop assistant in a clothes shop. Do you like this job?
Candidate A:	I don't know. I haven't thought about it before. Maybe you can get cheap clothes if you work in a shop!
Candidate B:	Yes, maybe! But I think it's hard work. You probably get very tired serving people all day. This picture shows a musician. I think it's a good job, but you must be very good at playing an instrument. What do you think?
Candidate A:	Yes! You must be very good and you have to practise a lot. And the last picture is a business person. I'd love that job. What about you?

Candidate B:	I don't share your opinion. I don't want to be a business person. Being in business is hard work and I don't think I'd be good at it.
Examiner:	Candidate A, why do you think being a business person is a good job?
Candidate A:	I think you can make a lot of money if you're good at it. You could start your own business, work hard and become rich.
Examiner:	Candidate B, you said you don't want to be a business person because it's hard work. Is there anything else you don't like about this job?
Candidate B:	Well, you have to go to a lot of meetings and you have to wear a suit. Your boss checks your work all the time, and you have to sell, sell, sell, all the time.
Examiner:	So, Candidate A, which of these jobs do you like the best?
Candidate A:	I think a business person has the best job.
Examiner:	And you, Candidate B, which of these jobs do you like the best?
Candidate B:	I think a doctor has the best job.
Examiner:	Thank you. Can I have the booklet, please?
	Now, Candidate B, can you compare working in a library with working as a shop assistant?
Candidate B:	In both jobs you have to talk to people. In a shop you have to take people's money and in a library you have to help people with their books.
Examiner:	And what about you, Candidate A? Can you compare a musician with a doctor?
Candidate A:	In my opinion, they're both good jobs and they're both difficult. You have to spend a long time studying and practising before you can be a musician or a doctor. I think lots of people would like to do these jobs, but only a few will be successful.
Examiner:	Candidate A, which of these jobs are you least interested in doing?
Candidate A:	I wouldn't be interested in working in a shop.
Examiner:	Why not?
Candidate A:	I think it's boring and very tiring.
Examiner:	Which of these jobs are you least interested in, Candidate B?
Candidate B:	I wouldn't like to work in a shop either. I want to do something more interesting in my life.
Examiner:	Thank you. That is the end of the test.

Test 8

Speaking Part 1

🎧
55a

Examiner:	Good afternoon.
	Can I have your mark sheets, please?
	I'm Keira Benn. And this is Noel Connor.
	What's your name, Candidate A?
Candidate A:	My name's Apinya Saengsawang.
Examiner:	And what's your name, Candidate B?
Candidate B:	My name's Omar Saleh.
Examiner:	Candidate B, how old are you?
Candidate B:	I'm twelve.
Examiner:	Where are you from, Candidate B?
Candidate B:	I'm from Jordan.
Examiner:	Thank you.
	Candidate A, how old are you?
Candidate A:	I'm thirteen.
Examiner:	Where are you from?
Candidate A:	I'm from Thailand.
Examiner:	Thank you.
	Now, let's talk about festivals.
	Candidate A, what is an important festival where you come from?

Candidate A:	Songkran Festival is important in Thailand. It's also called the water festival and it's the start of the new year in Thailand.
Examiner:	What do you do at Songkran?
Candidate A:	We clean our houses before the festival and during the festival people throw water at each other.
Examiner:	Candidate B, what is an important festival in your country?
Candidate B:	Eid is the most important festival in Jordan.
Examiner:	What do you do during this festival, Candidate B?
Candidate B:	Family is very important. The whole family comes together and we see our cousins, uncles and aunts. There are a lot of delicious things to eat and everybody wears their best clothes.
Examiner:	Now, Candidate A, please tell me what you like best about your favourite festival.
Candidate A:	Well, the water festival is my favourite. The best thing about it is playing with the water. You get very wet and have a lot of fun. Everywhere you go, people throw water, so you don't wear your best clothes! There's delicious food to eat as well.
Examiner:	Now, let's talk about going to the cinema. Candidate B, do you often go to the cinema?
Candidate B:	Yes, I do.
Examiner:	What kind of films do you watch, Candidate B?
Candidate B:	I like exciting films, so I really enjoy action films. For example, I saw all the Mission Impossible films at the cinema.
Examiner:	Candidate A, do you often go to the cinema?
Candidate A:	No, I don't.
Examiner:	Why not?
Candidate A:	My friends and I prefer to watch a film at home because the cinema is expensive. If you watch a film at home, you can talk to your friends about it at the same time.
Examiner:	Now, Candidate B, can you tell me about the last time you went to the cinema?
Candidate B:	Yes. I think it was six months ago. I went with my friends, but I can't remember the film we saw. We went together in the afternoon because the weather was bad and we couldn't do anything outdoors. Afterwards, we went for a snack and a drink and we had a very nice time.
Examiner:	Thank you.

Speaking Part 2

🎧
56a

Examiner:	Now, in this part of the test you are going to talk together. Here are some pictures that show different pets. Do you like these different pets? Say why or why not. I'll say that again. Do you like these different pets? Say why or why not. All right? Now, talk together.
Candidate A:	I think this picture shows a rabbit, and in my opinion, it's a good pet for a young child. Do you think a rabbit is a good pet?
Candidate B:	Yes, I do. I think you can pick up a rabbit and hold it and play with it. The next picture shows mice. I think a mouse would be like a rabbit, but smaller. What do you think about mice as pets?
Candidate A:	Mice might be good if you don't have a lot of space at home because they're small, but I don't think they're very interesting pets. You can watch them go around in their wheel, but they don't do much – and some people don't like mice!
Candidate B:	That's true. My sister hates mice!
Candidate A:	What about a dog?
Candidate B:	Oh! A dog! I think a dog is a really good pet. You can make really good friends with a dog.
Candidate A:	Yes, that's right, and you can play with it. You can throw a ball and it will bring it back to you.
Candidate B:	You can also teach it to do lots of other things. Now, here's a picture of a cat. Would you like to have a pet cat?

Candidate A:	Yes, I would, if it's a friendly cat. Some cats aren't very friendly.
Candidate B:	The last picture shows chickens. I think it's strange to have chickens as pets.
Candidate A:	Yes, I agree with you. People keep chickens for their eggs, but I don't think they're really pets.
Candidate B:	Well, maybe some people keep them as pets.
Candidate A:	Yes, but I don't think I want to play with a chicken.
Examiner:	Candidate A, you said a rabbit is a good pet for a young child. Why?
Candidate A:	I think it's easy to look after a rabbit. You just have to give it some food and clean water and clean its home.
Examiner:	Candidate B, you didn't say what you thought about having a mouse as a pet. Can you tell us now?
Candidate B:	I think a mouse is a good pet. You can take it out of its cage and hold it. It can sit in your hands and run up your arms. I think mice are fun.
Examiner:	So, Candidate A, which of these pets do you like the best?
Candidate A:	I think a dog is the best pet because you can have the most fun with it.
Examiner:	And you, Candidate B, which of these pets do you like the best?
Candidate B:	I also think a dog is the best – for the same reason.
Examiner:	Thank you. Can I have the booklet, please? Now, Candidate B, can you compare having a rabbit with having chickens?
Candidate B:	Yes. Chickens are more useful because they give you eggs. I think it would be fun to go and collect the eggs every day. You can't keep chickens or rabbits inside your house. I think they have to live outside. A rabbit is a quiet pet, but I think chickens are noisy.
Examiner:	And what about you, Candidate A? Can you compare having a cat with having a mouse?
Candidate A:	They're very different pets. A cat doesn't always stay at home, so it'll go outside on its own. But a mouse has to stay in its cage all the time. You can take it out and play with it, but it might run away and you might lose it. You can also play with a cat, especially when it's young. The best thing about a cat is that it will sit on you and make you feel comfortable. You can't do that with a mouse. If you take it out of the cage, you have to watch it all the time.
Examiner:	Candidate A, which of these pets do you think is the worst?
Candidate A:	I think the chickens are the worst. You can't really do anything with them.
Examiner:	Which of these pets do you think is the worst, Candidate B?
Candidate B:	I agree that chickens are the worst pets. I don't really think they are pets.
Examiner:	Thank you. That is the end of the test.

Speaking: Additional practice by topic

This section will give you extra practice in answering the sorts of questions the examiner may ask you in Part 1 of the Speaking test. Listen to the audio and practise answering the questions. Some of the questions are similar but the words used in the question are different; this gives you more speaking practice and shows you how different questions are formed. Remember in this part of the test, the examiner will ask you some questions on everyday topics and the examiner will choose what questions to ask you and won't ask you lots of questions about the same topic.

Try to give answers of two or more sentences. Don't just answer 'yes' or 'no'. The examiner wants to hear you speaking English and if you just say 'yes' or 'no', this doesn't help them understand how well you speak it. Answer the examiner's question in the first sentence and explain your answer a bit more in the second sentence. Here is an example question and answer:

Examiner: Do you like going to the cinema?

Student: Yes, I do. Going to the cinema is one of my favourite activities. I really like horror films.

Once you are feeling confident it would be a good idea not to look at the book – just listen to the audio and answer the questions. Also look at the **How to prepare for the test** and **Model answers for Speaking** sections of the book for good example answers to Part 1 Speaking questions. And keep practising!

The questions below are grouped under the topics that you should be able to talk about: Clothes, Daily life, Entertainment and media, Food and drink, Health, medicine and exercise, Hobbies and leisure, House and home, Language, Opinions and experiences, People, Personal feelings, Personal identification, Places and buildings, School and study, Services, Shopping, Social interaction, Sport, The natural world, Transport, Travel and holidays, Weather.

Clothes

57

Now let's talk about clothes.
Where do you buy your clothes?
Can you describe your school uniform?
What sort of clothes do you wear at the weekend?
What are your most comfortable clothes?
What clothes do you wear if you are staying at home all day?
Do you like looking at clothes in shops?
What sort of shoes do you usually wear?
Do you and your parents sometimes have different opinions about what you should wear?
Do you follow fashion in clothes?
Do you think it is important to wear clothes that are in fashion?
Are your clothes always new? Or do you sometimes get them from somebody else, like an older brother or sister?
Do you have any special clothes that you only wear when you want to look nice? When do you wear them? Describe them.

Daily life
58

Now let's talk about daily life.
What time do you get up in the morning?
What's the first thing you do in the morning?
What do you do before you go to school in the morning?
What do you have for lunch?
What do you do when you finish school?
What do you have for dinner?
What time do you usually go to bed?
What do you do before you go to sleep?
Do you have to help around the house? What do you have to do?
Do your parents give you money every week to spend on yourself? What do you spend it on?

Do you have any neighbours? What are they like?
Do you have any pets?
How often do you see your friends?

Entertainment and media

59

Now let's talk about things you like to watch and listen to.
How often do you watch television?
What is your favourite television programme?
Do you have a mobile phone? What do you use it for?
Do you watch things on television, on a computer or on your mobile phone?
What kind of music do you listen to?
Do you play any musical instruments?
Do you like dancing?
Do you ever go to music concerts?
Do you often go to the cinema?
What sort of films do you like?
Tell us about the last film you saw at the cinema.
Do you use social media? What famous people do you follow?

Food and drink

60

Now let's talk about food and drink.
What do you usually have for breakfast?
If you are hungry at home, what do you have as a snack?
What's your favourite food?
What food don't you like?
What fruit and vegetables do you eat?
Can you cook anything?
Do you like fast food?
Do you and your family often eat out at restaurants?
Which drinks do you like?
Do you eat lots of sweets?
Are there any dishes that you have on special holidays? What are they?

Health, medicine and exercise

61

Now let's talk about being healthy and fit.
What do you think is the best way to keep fit?
What do you do to keep fit?
How often do you exercise?
What food do you eat that is good for you?
What sports do you do?
Do you often get ill?
Tell us about the last time you were ill.
Have you ever had to take medicine? When?
How often do you go to the dentist?
Tell us about the last time you went to the dentist.
Have you ever had an accident and hurt yourself? What happened?

Hobbies and leisure

62

Now let's talk about what you do in your free time.
What's your favourite hobby?
What do you do in your free time?
What do you do in the evenings after school?
How do you spend your weekends?
What's your favourite way to spend your weekends?
Are there any hobbies that you would like to try?

Have you started any new hobbies in the last few months or years?
What hobbies do people in your family have?
Do you think playing a musical instrument is a good hobby? Why/Why not?
Do your parents ever suggest hobbies to you? Which ones?
Do you think you have enough free time?
When is your leisure time?
Do you think young people spend too much of their free time on their mobile phones?

House and home

63

Now let's talk about where you live.
Tell us about the area where you live.
Please describe your home.
Can you describe the building that you live in?
Describe your bedroom.
Do you share your bedroom with a brother or sister?
Which is your favourite room in your home?
Describe your living room to us.
Describe your perfect home.
Is there anything you would like to change about your home?
Who lives with you in your home?

Language

64

Now let's talk about languages that you speak.
What languages do you speak? How well do you speak them?
Are you good at learning languages?
What languages would you like to speak?
When did you start learning English?
Do you like learning English?
Do you think English is a difficult language to learn? Why/Why not?
What's the hardest thing about learning English?
How often do you practise speaking English?
Is it important to learn English? Why?
What do you think is the best way to learn a language?

Opinions and experiences

65

Now let's talk about your opinions and experiences.
Tell us about the last time you got a present that you liked.
Tell us about a time when you did a favour for somebody.
Have you ever had to go to hospital? Can you tell us about it?
Tell us about a time when you felt very happy.
Tell us about a time when you felt angry.
Do you ever worry about things? What sort of things?
Do you ever get bored? When?
What places in the world would you like to visit?
Describe the best holiday you've ever had.
Describe the best experience you've ever had.
Describe the funniest or scariest thing that's ever happened to you.

People

66

Now let's talk about people.
Describe a member of your family.

Do you have any brothers or sisters? What are they like?
Tell us about your grandparents.
Do you have any aunts, uncles and cousins?
How often do you see your grandparents?
How often do you see your aunts, uncles and cousins?
What's your best friend like? Describe them.
What's important in a friend?
Tell us about a famous person you like.
Who is your favourite sports star? Why do you like them?
Who is your favourite singer? Why do you like them?
Who is your favourite actor? Why do you like them?
Which famous person would you like to meet? Why?
What sort of people do you like?
What sort of people don't you like?

Personal feelings

67

Now let's talk about personal feelings.
How are you feeling today?
Do you often get angry? What things make you angry?
What things make you happy?
Where and when do you feel happiest?
What makes you feel good?
What kind of things make you feel bored?
What makes you feel sad?
What do you do when you feel unhappy?
Who do you talk to if you have a problem?
Tell us about a time when you had a problem and you didn't know what to do.
What do you do if your friend has a problem or is unhappy?
What things are you scared of?
What do you do when you are scared?
Do you worry a lot?
What things do you worry about?

Personal identification

68

Now let's talk about you.
Tell us about your family.
Do you think you are like your parents?
How would your friends describe you?
Describe somebody who is important to you.
What do you like about your home country?
What are people from your country like?
What things in life are most important to you?
Is money important to you?
What do you want to be when you grow up?
What would you like to do when you finish school?
Have you changed since you were a young child? How have you changed?
Do you think you are a lucky person? Why/Why not?

Places and buildings

69

Now let's talk about places and buildings.
Describe your home town.
What things in your home town would you show to visitors?

What do you like about the place where you live?
What is your country famous for?
What is your city or town famous for?
What do tourists like to do when they visit your country?
What famous buildings are there in your town, city or country?
Where would you like to live if you could live anywhere in the world?
What do you like to do when you visit a new place?
Would you prefer to live in the city or the countryside? Why?
Describe a famous building that you have visited.
What's your favourite place to go on holiday?
Describe a place where you feel very happy.

School and study

70

Now let's talk about school and studying.
Tell us about your favourite teacher.
Describe one of your teachers to us.
Tell us about your journey to school.
What do you like best about going to school?
What don't you like about your school?
What's your favourite subject?
What subjects do you like? Why do you like them?
What subjects don't you like? Why don't you like them?
Tell us about your school day.
What do you do during lunchtime at your school?
Would you like to go to university? Why/Why not?
Do you have a lot of tests and exams at school?
Do you have to do a lot of homework?
Do you think students have too much homework?

Services

71

Now let's talk about the places and shops in your town or city.
Is there a supermarket near your home? How do you get to it?
Is there a library near your home?
Are there any interesting museums in your town or city?
Are there any good restaurants near your home?
Is there a swimming pool in the area where you live?
Is there anywhere for children to play near your home?
Can you do sports near your home? Which ones?
Do you live near a hospital?
Do you have to travel a long way to see a doctor or a dentist?
What shops are there near your home?
Can you easily post a letter where you live?
Can you catch a bus or a train easily from your home to travel somewhere else?

Shopping

72

Now let's talk about shopping.
Do you like shopping? Why/Why not?
What are your favourite shops?
Do you like shopping for clothes?
Do you ever go food shopping?
Do you go shopping with your friends? Where do you go and what do you buy?
Do you like spending time in shopping centres?
What did you buy the last time you went shopping?

What do you like spending your money on?
Do you ever spend too much money when you go shopping?
Tell us about a present you bought for somebody.

Social interaction

73

Now let's talk about friends.
Do you have a lot of friends?
Do you find it easy to make friends?
Do you like chatting to people?
What's a good way to make new friends?
Are friends important to you? Why?
What's important in a friend?
Tell us about your best friend.
What do you like doing with your friends?
What do you talk about with your friends?
Who's your oldest friend?
Do you talk to your parents a lot? What do you talk to them about?
Do you talk with your family at meal times?

Sport

74

Now let's talk about sport.
What sports do you like watching?
Are you a sports fan?
Do you enjoy playing sports? Which ones?
Are you good at sports? Which ones?
Are there any sports you aren't good at?
What sports do you play at school?
Are you in a sports team? Tell us about it.
Do you play sports with your friends outside school? Which ones? Where do you play them?
Which important sporting events do you like watching?
Do you like watching events like the Olympic Games?
Tell us about a sport that you don't like.
What sports would you like to try?

The natural world

75

Now let's talk about nature.
Do you enjoy being outside? Why/Why not?
Do you enjoy being in the countryside? Why/Why not?
What outdoor activities do you enjoy doing?
Do you enjoy going for walks outside?
Are there any green spaces where you live? Describe them.
Where can you go to enjoy nature?
What activities can people do in nature where you live?
What have you learned about nature at school?
Is it important to learn about nature? Why/Why not?
Do people need to look after nature?
What can we do to look after nature?

Transport, travel and holidays

76

Now let's talk about transport, travel and holidays.
What types of transport do you usually use?
Which is the best form of transport, in your opinion?
Which is the worst form of transport, in your opinion?

Does your town or city have good transport?
Is it easy to travel from your home to other places?
What's the most exciting journey you've ever been on? Describe it.
Have you ever been to another country? Tell us about it.
How do you spend your time during the school holidays?
What kind of holidays do you enjoy?
Tell us about your last holiday.

Weather

77

Now let's talk about the weather.
What's the weather like in your country in summer?
What's the weather like in your country in winter?
What's the weather like in your country in the different seasons?
What sort of weather do you like?
Does it rain a lot in your country? Do you like the rain? Why/Why not?
Do you need to be careful of the sun in your country?
What summer activities do you like doing?
What winter activities do you like doing?
Have you ever played in snow?
Does the weather change how you feel?
Do you feel happier in the winter or the summer?
Which is your favourite season? Why?